Anonymous

Proceedings of the College Section

of the Illinois state teachers' association. 1887-88

Anonymous

Proceedings of the College Section
of the Illinois state teachers' association. 1887-88

ISBN/EAN: 9783337254568

Printed in Europe, USA, Canada, Australia, Japan

Cover: Foto ©ninafisch / pixelio.de

More available books at **www.hansebooks.com**

PROCEEDINGS

—:OF THE:—

COLLEGE SECTION

— OF THE —

ILLINOIS

STATE TEACHERS' ASSOCIATION.

SPRINGFIELD.

December 27 and 28, 1888.

UNIVERSITY PRESS CO. EVANSTON ILL

CONTENTS.

	PAGE.
Constitution	3
Record of Proceedings	4
Address by the President, Selim H. Peabody, Ph. D., LL. D., Regent of the University of Illinois	9
Paper by Joseph R. Harker, Principal of Whipple Academy, Jacksonville: "What are we Doing in this State to Prepare Pupils for College?"	14
Paper by H. A. Fischer, A. M., Professor of Mathematics in Wheaton College: "Uniform Courses in Colleges."	25
Paper by Rev. H. F. Fisk, D. D., Professor of Pedagogics, Northwestern University: "How can our School Programmes be Shortened and Enriched?"	34
Paper by Rev. J. B. McMichael, D. D., President of Monmouth College: "Limitation of State Provision for Education."	51
Paper by Rev. W. C. Roberts, D. D., LL. D., President of Lake Forest University: "Education."	61
Paper by Rev. Nathaniel Butler, Jr., A. M., Professor of Latin, University of Illinois: "Purposes of the Study of Latin."	76
Paper by Rev. E. A. Tanner, D. D., President of Illinois College, Jacksonville: "The College Phase of the New Education."	92

CONSTITUTION.

ARTICLE I.

This association shall be called the College Section of the Illinois State Teachers' Association.

ARTICLE II.

All instructors of the universities, colleges, and seminaries of the State of Illinois shall be entitled to membership in this association, provided that they are members of the State Teachers' Association.

ARTICLE III.

The officers of the College Section shall consist of a President, Vice-President, Secretary, and an Executive Committee of three, who shall be elected by ballot at each annual meeting.

ARTICLE IV.

It shall be the duty of the Executive Committee to make all necessary arrangements for the meetings of the College Section, including programme, papers, and topics for discussion.

PROCEEDINGS.

FIRST ANNUAL MEETING, DECEMBER 28, 1887.

MORNING SESSION.

Twenty-one members of college faculties of the State of Illinois met pursuant to call at ten o'clock in the Supreme Court Room of the Capitol at Springfield, December 28, 1887.

The meeting was called to order by Professor J. C. Hutchison, of Monmouth College. Professor G. R. Cutting, of Lake Forest University, was appointed Temporary Secretary.

The committee appointed at Chicago last Summer on organization of a College Section — Professor J. C. Hutchison, of Monmouth College; President E. A. Tanner, of Illinois College, and Professor D. A. Straw, of Wheaton College, — presented a report recommending an organization and proposing a constitution.

Moved by President E. A. Tanner, of Illinois College, that such an association as that proposed by the committee be formed. Carried.

Regent S. H. Peabody, of the State University, Professor L. F. Griffin, of Lake Forest University, and Professor R. Nutting, of Blackburn University, were appointed a committee to confer with the Executive Committee of the Illinois State Teachers' Association relative to the formation of this body as a section of the State Association.

The Section then listened to a paper by Professor E. F. Reid, of Monmouth College, on "Some defects in Our Colleges and the Means of Their Removal." A copy was requested for publication.

Adjourned till 3 P. M.

AFTERNOON SESSION.

College Section met at 3 P. M. Minutes approved.

Regent S. H. Peabody, of the Committee on Conference, reported that a resolution would be introduced into the State Association favoring the introduction of the College Section into the State Association.

The constitution, as found on page 4, was read, considered, and unanimously adopted.

The following were appointed a Committee on Nominations: President M. D. Hornbeck, of Chaddock College; Professor J. W. Jenks, of Knox College, and Professor R. Nutting, of Blackburn University.

This committee reported a list of officers as follows: President, S. H. Peabody, LL. D., Regent of University of Illinois; Vice President, Rev. E. A. Tanner, D. D., President of Illinois College; Secretary, Professor G. R. Cutting, of Lake Forest University; Executive Committee — Professor J. C. Hutchison, of Monmouth College; Professor Robert D. Sheppard, D. D., of Northwestern University, and Professor G. R. Cutting, of Lake Forest University. The above were elected by ballot.

A paper was then read by President Charles A. Blanchard, of Wheaton College, on the "Relation of the College to the Common School." It was voted to request its publication. A discussion followed.

Adjourned to meet in joint session with the State Association, subject to call of the Executive Committee.

G. R. CUTTING, *Secretary*.

SECOND ANNUAL MEETING.

FIRST SESSION, DECEMBER 27, 1888.

The College Section was called to order by President S. H. Peabody at 2:30 P. M.

Prayer was offered by Dr. E. L. Hurd, of Blackburn University.

An opening address was delivered by President S. H. Peabody. (See page 9.)

Principal J. R. Harker, of Jacksonville, read a paper on "What are we Doing in this State to Prepare Pupils for College?" (See page 14.)

Professor H. A. Fischer, of Wheaton, read a paper on "Uniform Courses in Colleges." (See page 25.)

After discussion a committee was appointed to consider all matters proposed in this paper and report next year, as follows: Regent S H. Peabody of the State University, President W. C. Roberts, of Lake Forest University, President E. L. Hurd, of Blackburn University, President E. A. Tanner, of Illinois College, and Professor H. A. Fischer, of Wheaton College.

Professor H. F. Fisk, of Northwestern University, read a paper, "How can our School Programmes be Shortened and Enriched?" (See page 34.) Discussion followed.

Professor J. C. Hutchison then read a paper prepared by Rev. J. B. McMichael, D. D., President of Monmouth College. (See page 51.)

The following committees were appointed: Nominations — Professor George Churchill, of Knox College; Professor Levi Seeley, of Lake Forest University, and Professor D. A. Straw, of Wheaton College; Publication of Papers— Professor G. R. Cutting, of Lake Forest University; Professor J. C. Hutchison, of Monmouth College, and Professor Holmes Dysinger, of Carthage College.

Adjourned till 2 P. M. Friday.

G. R. CUTTING, *Secretary.*

SECOND SESSION, December 28, 1888.

The College Section was called to order by President S. H. Peabody, at 2.30 p. m.

Prayer was offered by President E. A. Tanner, of Illinois College.

The Committee on Publication made a report favoring the printing of the transactions of the College Section.

The publication of the transactions and papers of the College Section was referred to the Executive Committee for 1889 with authority to publish if they can provide for the expense.

A paper on "Education" was next presented by President W. C. Roberts, of Lake Forest University. (See page 61.)

Rev. Nathaniel Butler, Jr., A. M., Professor of Latin in the Illinois University, read a paper on "Purposes of the Study of Latin." (See page 76.)

President E. A. Tanner, of Illinois College, presented a paper on "The College Phase of the New Education." (See page 92.)

Elisha Gray, LL. D., of Highland Park, next delivered an address on "The Telautograph." A vote of thanks was tendered to Professor Gray for his address.

The Committee on Nominations proposed the following officers for 1889, and they were elected by ballot: President, W. C. Roberts, President of Lake Forest University; Vice-President, J. B. McMichael, President of Monmouth College; Secretary, J. R. Harker, Illinois College; Executive Committee — D. A. Straw, Wheaton College; H. F. Fisk, Northwestern University; and J. R. Harker, Illinois College.

Adjourned.

G. R. CUTTING, *Secretary.*

ADDRESS.

BY THE PRESIDENT OF THE SECTION, SELIM H. PEABODY, LL. D., REGENT OF THE UNIVERSITY OF ILLINOIS, CHAMPAIGN.

Gentlemen of the College Section:

For a term of years the sessions of the College Section of the State Teachers' Association of Illinois have been suspended. Whether this suspension was caused by any lack of interest on the part of the Section itself, or whether it happened because all division of the Association into sections was for a time abandoned, does not appear, and is probably of little consequence to us. It is certainly a reason for congratulation that the college men of the State have deemed it wise to resuscitate some form of organization, in which they may renew or form acquaintances, may join in friendly discussion of questions vital to their common work, and may give some fresh impetus to the grand and inspiring cause of higher education in Illinois and in the United States. I believe it also to be wise that this organization has taken pains to affiliate itself with the State Association, and to become an integral part thereof, rather than to stand aloof as a separate body. The educational interests of this land and of this State are, and they ought to be, so thoroughly in harmony, so inextricably and indissolubly interwoven as to unite all thought, all aspiration, all effort, in a common cause—and that cause is the advancement of the human race. As the several arms of military warfare have their proper services in each grand army, infantry, cavalry, artillery, and engineers, all aiding all, and each contending after his fashion in a thoroughly organized and united movement against a common enemy, so are the different departments, primary, secondary, and higher, including seminary and college, technical, and professional schools, but the different arms of the Grand Educational Army of the Republic. Their only rivalry should be the generous rivalry which strives to excel in doing the greatest good.

I find in the latest report of the State Superintendent of Public Instruction a list of educational institutions in Illinois incorporated by law, numbering ninety-seven. Of these, reports were made by only fifty-seven. Of these, there appear to be:

Professional and reformatory	10
Academies	12
Seminaries for women	13
Colleges for men, or for both sexes	22 — 57

It is probable that these are not exactly classified.

The latest report of the United States Commissioner of Education names twenty-five colleges, of which only eighteen are reported as conferring degrees at the commencements of 1886. The population of the State is about that of the United States at the close of the revolutionary war. The number of colleges now existing in the United States which were in existence at the close of that war is twelve; at the end of the last century, twenty-one. The ratio of colleges in this State now, and of the United States at the periods referred to, is not very different.

For the year ending at Commencement, 1886:

The number of college instructors was	233
Instructors in preparatory classes connected with colleges	46 — 279
The number of collegiate students was	1,629
The number of preparatory, professional, and other	3,028 — 4,657

The same report gives for the higher education of women:

Number of schools	9
Number of instructors	108
Number of students	973

Address of Dr. Selim H. Peabody.

The ratio of college students to population in the Northern Central States, including the area north of the Ohio River, and of the south line of Missouri and Kansas, is given at 1 : 1,273; but the ratio of college students in the State of Illinois for the year named, taking the population at 3,200,000 (3,180,354), will be 1 : 1,903. Applying the ratio first given, it would appear that about twenty-five hundred (2,514) Illinois students are somewhere in college, unless we admit, which we shall hardly be prepared to admit, that Illinois is furnishing fewer students for higher education than are her immediate neighbors. The neighboring States do not excel Illinois in any other signs of material prosperity, or intellectual advancement, and are not likely to excel her in this particular. It appears, then, that, while there are 1,630 students in Illinois colleges, about nine hundred Illinois students are somewhere else at college, or that only about two-thirds of the college students of the State are in their own schools. Of course, it is not possible in a matter like this to be exact, but other estimates of the same subject have led to the conclusion that fully one-third of our students go out of the State for their college education. An inspection of the catalogues of Harvard, Yale, Princeton, Cornell, the University of Michigan, and the Institute of Technology shows in each one a very considerable number of Illinois students, and this, too, in spite of the fact that the student who goes abroad incurs large cost for travel, tuition fees from two to ten times what he would pay at home, and expenses of living from two to fourfold his expenses at home.

There are reasons for all this.

First, the Eastern schools have in most instances the prestige of age. Their alumni are scattered all through our society, and the rule is that a college alumnus sends his boy where he himself graduated, if he can spare the money to do so.

Secondly, the Eastern schools have in numerous instances the prestige of large, and in some cases of magnificent, endowments; and endowments mean the power of increasing facilities of instruction, of securing the best talent, by both which means brilliant inducements to students who can meet the cost are offered. The institutions are not to be blamed for their past. It is their business to grow as fast and to become as powerful as they can. The students are not to be blamed. If I were a student planning to spend four years of the hey-dey of my life in college, with what of money would be needful for my support and instruction, I would get the very best that my money would buy, whether at home or away from home would not signify, and I should very likely be attracted by the glint of grand endowments and renowned instructors and magnificent equipments.

And when I meet an ingenuous youth, whose face, like the lad's in the second picture of Cole's Voyage of Life, is fixed intently on the glorious phantom resplendent in the eastern sky, I say to him: "Choose now distinctly what you wish to do — what kind of an education you seek to secure, and then find where you can get that the best. But before you finally decide, think how much of the result depends on yourself, how much more depends on yourself than upon your surroundings, and judge whether, after all, you may not really make the best of yourself under conditions less exacting and more in keeping with your means." I still rejoice that here in Illinois are open a goodly number of institutions, whence flow abundant founts of sound learning, at whose brim the earnest, ingenuous youth may drink his fill, even though poverty be his heritage and hard toil the cost of his daily bread. Many a poor boy struggled through his college life in New England forty years ago who would find to-day the odds too great to be borne.

My brethren of the College Guild, there is no doubt that in our efforts to found colleges here in the West that shall be, when they are as old, what the Eastern colleges have come to be, we are striving against great odds. But there is need here for us, all of us, and more. This broad, rich, grand prairie State, the Empire State of the central land, with its teeming population, its grand position, its exuberant wealth, has need for all the culture, all the science, all the refinement, all the discipline, that can be developed by the cordial, combined, and efficient labors of the faithful laborers who are giving the best efforts of their lives to found and perpetuate colleges in her midst.

Each of us, in his own view, is poor. What is poverty but the lack of means to satisfy our wants? Our poverty consists in this, that we discover so many and so important and so useful purposes ready for our efforts if we had but the means to accomplish them. Dr. Angell once said to me that the normal condition of every active educational institution is to be in want, and that Michigan University was too poor to fulfill her mission.

There remains to us our work. Which, elsewhere, is the earnest performance of our duties towards our students, the public, and sound learning; and here, to discuss, with I am sure the kindest harmony, questions of importance to our common weal.

WHAT ARE WE DOING IN ILLINOIS TO PREPARE STUDENTS FOR COLLEGE?

BY JOSEPH R. HARKER, PRINCIPAL OF WHIPPLE ACADEMY, JACKSONVILLE, ILLINOIS.

In order to secure definite information on the subject of this paper, I sent circulars of inquiry to the colleges, academies, and high schools of the state. The colleges were requested to analyze their Freshman classes of the present year, with a view to ascertain where the students received their preparation for college. The academies and high schools were asked to report the extent of their courses of study, and the number of their graduates that have gone to college in the past four years. I am under obligations to 11 colleges, 11 academies, and 83 high schools; and personally thank all my correspondents for their promptness and courtesy. Many of them not only gave the information wanted in the way of statistics, but also freely expressed their views on the general subject of preparation for college, so that I am able in this paper to present, in the way of suggestion, the views of many besides myself.

Comparing the reports from the colleges, we find that most of our college students are prepared by the colleges themselves. Ewing College prepared all its Freshman class; Illinois College, about 90 per cent.; Illinois Wesleyan, 75 per cent.; Knox and Lake Forest have recently made changes in their requirements, so that no definite figures could be given, but the percentage is high; Northwestern University, 50 per cent.; University of Illinois, not definitely stated, but I judge from the report about 40 per cent. It is safe to conclude that on the average 75 per cent. of our college students are prepared by the colleges themselves in their preparatory classes.

Of the remaining 25 per cent., a careful study of the reports from colleges and high schools seems to show that 20 per cent. come from the high schools, and about 5 per cent. from academies and seminaries not connected with the colleges.

This general summary of the reports received will serve as a basis for a few observations.

1. Practically all that we are doing in Illinois to prepare students for college is done by the colleges themselves.

Colleges were founded early in the history of our state by earnest men and women who believed that in the beginnings of colonization an opportunity should be given for the complete development of the faculties of man, and that the foundations of stable governments could be laid only in liberal learning and in Christian character. They laid the foundations of the higher education wisely, and with unfaltering faith and unflinching devotion they and their successors have builded thereupon, so that to-day we have a number of institutions of higher learning of which any state may justly be proud. But it has been an arduous task to accomplish this result. The friends of the colleges have had not only to carry on college work, to secure endowments and funds for that work, but also to provide their own materials. Like the Israelites in Egypt, they have not only made brick, but they have been obliged to gather their own straw. There is not a college in the state that has found it possible to carry on its own work without the aid of a preparatory department to provide college material. In almost every instance the number of students in this preparatory department is greater than the number in the college courses. The time and strength of the professors have been divided, and in many cases by far the greater part of their work has been to give secondary instruction. They have not taken up this kind of work from choice, but from necessity. It has been impossible to secure students already prepared.

The colleges have constantly protested against this necessity. As early as 1838, the trustees of the Illinois College at Jacksonville adopted a resolution to dispense with the preparatory department. But they soon found themselves compelled to take up the work again. So also with other colleges. They have limited the time given to preparatory work as much as possible, making it only one year, and trying to crowd the necessary preparation within that limit; but they have found this in most cases altogether inadequate, and have been forced to arrange for complete courses of secondary instruction. The State University, perhaps more than any other institution, has endeavored to secure students without arranging a preparatory class. Its natural position, as the head of the state system of public schools, gives it exceptional advantages in this respect. But it is compelled, year by year, in spite of its constant protests, to maintain such a class, and to prepare a large percentage of its own students.

I think there is not a college faculty in the state who would not hail with delight the day when they could receive their students already prepared for college work.

But in the past, and to a large extent in the present, these preparatory departments of the colleges have been and are, as far as design goes, the only nurseries for higher education in the state. They make preparation for college their main work; the student in them is surrounded by influences tending strongly towards a college course; the teachers in these departments go out among the people as apostles of the higher education; and it does not take a long experience to teach any man who thus goes out among the people of the state that the colleges themselves, aided by their own preparatory departments, are almost the only forces aiming in this direction. That a college sentiment is growing, and, I believe, growing rapidly, is due, first, to their earnest persistence; secondly, to the fact that the public school men are beginning to aid in this work; and, thirdly, to the fact that in spite of Senator Ingalls the people are beginning to see that higher education does bring higher success in every department of life.

It is true also that hitherto the colleges have worked separately, and very little in combination. They have worked apart, each in his own section. That so much has been accomplished single-handed gives us great hope that, now a union has been effected, the growth of college spirit and of a belief in the utility of college education will be greatly quickened.

2. What of the high schools in this matter of college education?

As has been said, about 20 per cent. of the college students in the state enter directly from high schools. There are 169 high schools in the state, 5 of them reporting a five-years' course of study ; 70 a four years' course; and 94 a three years' course. They claim, as a rule, to require for entrance a fair knowledge of the common branches, the completion of the grammar grade work in the lower schools. Last year they graduated 1962 pupils. Of this number comparatively few attend college. Why?

Several reasons are given by my correspondents. One is that those who expect to go to college do not remain in the high school, but leave early to enter the preparatory department of whatever college they wish to attend.

Another is that most of the graduates are girls, and that, whether boys or girls, they have given as much time to education as they can afford, and must now begin life in some practical way.

Another is that the pupils find on graduation that they are not ready to enter college, and refuse to spend more time in preparation.

These reasons all have force, and require our attention ; but the main reason, to my mind, is in the popular conception of what the high school is. The general idea of the public, of teachers, of high school principals themselves, is, that the high schools are designed, not to prepare for a still higher education, but to complete the education of their students. Our high schools are a development of the lower common schools, and are independent of the colleges both in origin and design. The object of the common school has always been held to be preparation for practical life. The common schools originated in the necessities of the common people, and have developed with them. At first the course of instruction was very limited, embracing only reading, spelling, writing, and arithmetic; and little even of these. But as population and wealth increased, the course of study was enlarged, expanding to include the seven common branches, so-called, then adding algebra, geometry, the sciences, languages, then music, drawing, and so on, *ad libitum*. But with all the changes in development the purpose has not changed. When only the "three r's" were taught, and little even of these, the pupil was prepared for practical life; and now, at the end of the high school course, he reaches the same result.

The whole atmosphere of the high school tends to make the student satisfied with himself at graduation. Its course of study is arranged with the express purpose of fitting him for citizenship; and when he leaves the school, he leaves it feeling that now he is prepared for all life's duties; that a collegiate education may be a good thing, a luxury for those that can afford it, and that want it; but altogether unnecessary for practical life. The high school course is designed to finish the education of the pupil, and the teaching is done with that design in view. One principal says: "High school courses should be arranged on the idea that the school life ends there." Another says, "I consider the high school to be the top layer in our educational system." Another, "High schools should not be feeders to colleges, so few expect to go."

Such a conception of education is belittling to our profession.

To call any system of education complete short of the higher education smacks of demagoguery. In the history of our state the time has been when the poverty of the common people greatly limited their opportunities of education ; but the common people are all the people, and the proper conception of education for the people is, " Nothing short of the highest, unless necessity compels." If a boy must stop at the end of the primary grade, he must ; but let us not arrange for stopping there ; let us encourage him, and fit him, to go forward. If he must stop at the end of the grammar grade, he must ; but let us not arrange for stopping there ; let us encourage him, and fit him, to go forward. And in like manner, if a youth's education must end in the high school, we cannot avoid it ; but let us not deceive him by telling him he does not need more ; let us recognize and sympathize with his necessity, but let us so arrange the work that he will be encouraged, if opportunity offers, to go still higher.

The greatest educational need of Illinois to-day is a change of public opinion in regard to the utility of the higher education. This change must begin among the teachers of the public schools, and especially among the high school principals and teachers. I am glad to believe that such a change is now taking place, and that the sentiment is growing among high school men that the affiliations of the high school with the college should be more intimate.

Hitherto the relation between high schools and colleges has not been antagonistic—it has been merely indifferent. College teachers, as a class, are the product of the colleges ; high school teachers are the product of the public schools. The work of each class has been of an entirely different character, and they have not been brought together in any intimate way for the discussion of common educational questions. There has been a feeling, more or less vague, shared by both, that the public schools and the colleges exist for different purposes ; that they have little in common educationally; that the public schools exist for practical, everyday life, for the poor, for the "people"; and that the colleges exist for learned leisure, for the rich, for those above the people.

Separated thus in training, in methods of work, in aim, it is no wonder that they have been indifferent to each other. It ought to be said here in this College Section that for this relation of indifference the college men are mostly to blame. Their position at the higher end of the educational field gave them an outlook commanding the whole system; and they ought to have seen sooner that their highest success is possible only by the highest development of elementary and secondary instruction. But in some instances, instead of fostering and aiding general primary and secondary instruction, they have fought against it; they have been indifferent, and sometimes hostile, to the public school system generally, and to the high school in particular. It is well that college men should understand definitely that the public school system is a natural product of the American idea of government, and that the high school is a natural development of the public school system, and is here to stay.

High schools have in a great measure taken the place of the old-time academy. College men should see that all their students must come from the public schools; and they ought naturally to have taken up the public system with hearty sympathy, and to have aided in its development. And their highest interests to-day lie in the recognition of the high schools as their proper recruiting ground, and in co-operating to make these schools as perfect as may be.

We are just now learning much by a comparison of our system of education with that of Germany, confessing that in many respects we are far behind that country. It will be seen at once that the most distinctive feature of German schools is that the whole system is a unit, and that the primary and secondary courses of study are definitely arranged in the line of their University work. They have a single system; we have a double system. Our systems have no reference to each other; hardly fitting anywhere, in some parts overlapping, in others not reaching each other; and the result is necessarily waste of time, waste of energy, and disappointment in results. I believe the time has come for a general movement in the direction of uniting the high schools and the colleges in one common aim.

College men should favor such a movement because it will relieve them in part from the necessity of preparing nearly all their own students; and because with such an aim before our high schools, the belief in the necessity of a college education and the desire to attend college would be more general, and a larger number would seek admission.

I believe that high school men would favor such a movement. Some of them already urge very warmly that if the courses of study in the high schools were made to tend more in the direction of college work, the courses would then not only enable more pupils to go directly to college, but would be a better preparation for life than the present courses, even for those who cannot go on. Mr. Harvey, of Pittsfield, advocated this view in an able paper read last spring before the Central Illinois Teachers' Association at Galesburg, and many high school men there present agreed with him. Many of my correspondents express the same view.

It would require very little change in the present high school courses. Of the eighty-three high schools on my list, twelve have courses of study including two years or more of Greek and three years or more of Latin, enough to prepare students for the classical course in college, if the teacher is aiming in that direction. Forty-seven have three years or more of Latin, fifty-nine have two years or more of Latin; all have geometry from three to twelve months, averaging about eight months; all have algebra from six to fourteen months, averaging about ten months; all have higher

English studies, averaging about ten months; all have elementary science, averaging about twenty months. The only changes required would be the general recognition that the high school is not the end of the educational course, a little trimming of the studies here and there, and more definite teaching with a view to having the results accepted by college faculties.

Many high schools are anxious to make these changes, but find themselves greatly perplexed by the indefiniteness and want of uniformity of the admission requirements on the part of the colleges. It is next to impossible to prepare for college without having some definite college in mind. One college requires all of both plane and solid geometry, another no geometry at all; one requires little or no algebra, another a knowledge of quadratics and radicals; one is quite strict in admitting students, another is very lax. The colleges ought to have definite requirements; there ought to be substantial uniformity in our colleges in this respect; the requirements ought to conform as far as possible to the possibilities of the high schools; and the colleges ought to keep the high schools acquainted with their standard of requirements for admission.

The State University has done much to bring about such a connection as I urge, and is beginning to see some fruit to its labors. I am informed that the present year has brought it more students from high schools than ever before. But the State University alone should not do this; every college in the State should be working earnestly along the same line.

High school men would be glad of the added incentive such an arrangement would be to pupils to finish the high school course. Many pupils now leave the high school before graduation because the end of the course promises nothing definite.

I have no fear that such a union in purpose and idea as I have urged between colleges and high schools will injure any good academy in the state. A good academy will differ from a good high school not so much in its courses of study as in its more definitely religious aim and training. The high schools, belonging to all the people, take their students from all classes, and are hindered, as are all state institutions, from any but the most general religious influences. An academy, on the other hand, is usually founded for definite religious instruction; and while few are narrowly sectarian, nearly all are managed with a view to making religious training and Christian character fully as prominent as their literary instruction. Parents who desire such religious training and influences will always be found; and it will be true that every advance in the direction of the higher education will increase the means and the demand for good academies. There are now in Illinois some such academies, doing good work, but greatly hindered by public indifference in regard to the higher education. Owing to this indifference, many of the academies of the state are merely business schools, assuming or retaining the name for business purposes. They do not make much effort to prepare for a higher education. They find that the idea of getting what they call a practical education, and preparing for life in a few months, is in the air, is on the people, epidemic; and they arrange their courses so as to secure the largest possible patronage. I do not find that such academies send as many students to college, on the average, as do the high schools.

These schools and the so-called business colleges are a great injury to the higher education. They live on the weakness of the people; they invent arguments, and keep them constantly before the people, to show that it is unnecessary to spend years in securing an education. They are largely responsible for the idea that it is now possible to educate a boy in much less time than formerly, owing to improved methods, of which they seem to have a monopoly; and by their unwarranted assumption of the name of college, they lower the popular conception of the aim and standard of the higher education. A college is a college, in popular estimation; and it would aid greatly in giving clear conceptions of the educational system, if we could succeed in keeping the terms academy, college and university away from things that have no right to such names.

UNIFORM COURSES IN COLLEGES.

BY HERMAN A. FISCHER, A. M., PROFESSOR OF MATHEMATICS AND NATURAL PHILOSOPHY, WHEATON COLLEGE, WHEATON, ILL.

Mr. President, Ladies and Gentlemen:

A very learned essay is said to have been written on the theme, "Snakes in Ireland," beginning with the sentence: "There are no snakes in Ireland." This paper might, with equal propriety, begin with the sentence: "There are no uniform courses in colleges." There is sufficient variety to suit all tastes, but there is little or no harmony in the variety.

In preparing this paper, I consulted the catalogues of twenty-nine different colleges and universities, including twenty-one from our own State, all that were furnished in answer to my request; one from Beloit, just across the line; and the rest from the college of New Jersey, Oberlin and Williams Colleges, and Michigan, Wisconsin, Yale and Harvard Universities. In these catalogues, or calendars, nearly a dozen different courses are named, not including the various technical and professional courses. There is a classical course (also called ancient classical) and a modern classical course; there is a scientific course, a course in general science, a Latin scientific, a Greek scientific, and an English scientific course, a philosophical course, an English course, and so on.

The list of all the degrees conferred in these twenty-nine institutions is as puzzling as it is long. A young man who longs for distinction of this kind can, in the course of six or eight years, accumulate a string of initials to append to his name as long as the tail of a kite. He can begin with the degree Laureate of En-

higher education. A college is a college, in popular estimation; and it would aid greatly in giving clear conceptions of the educational system, if we could succeed in keeping the terms academy, college and university away from things that have no right to such names.

UNIFORM COURSES IN COLLEGES.

BY HERMAN A. FISCHER, A. M., PROFESSOR OF MATHEMATICS AND NATURAL PHILOSOPHY, WHEATON COLLEGE, WHEATON, ILL.

Mr. President, Ladies and Gentlemen:

A very learned essay is said to have been written on the theme, "Snakes in Ireland," beginning with the sentence: "There are no snakes in Ireland." This paper might, with equal propriety, begin with the sentence: "There are no uniform courses in colleges." There is sufficient variety to suit all tastes, but there is little or no harmony in the variety.

In preparing this paper, I consulted the catalogues of twenty-nine different colleges and universities, including twenty-one from our own State, all that were furnished in answer to my request; one from Beloit, just across the line; and the rest from the college of New Jersey, Oberlin and Williams Colleges, and Michigan, Wisconsin, Yale and Harvard Universities. In these catalogues, or calendars, nearly a dozen different courses are named, not including the various technical and professional courses. There is a classical course (also called ancient classical) and a modern classical course; there is a scientific course, a course in general science, a Latin scientific, a Greek scientific, and an English scientific course, a philosophical course, an English course, and so on.

The list of all the degrees conferred in these twenty-nine institutions is as puzzling as it is long. A young man who longs for distinction of this kind can, in the course of six or eight years, accumulate a string of initials to append to his name as long as the tail of a kite. He can begin with the degree Laureate of English literature; then for a few years further study he has the choice of twelve different baccalaureate degrees presented to him; after a few years of honorable existence he can become a master with his choice of six different letters, or syllables, to qualify the "M."; or he may continue his technical studies in one of four lines and become an Engineer; finally he may advance to the rank of Doctor, either by studying medicine or by getting into the good graces of some college board of trustees and having them "surprise" him with one or more of four honorary doctorates.

The American college confers as many as thirty different degrees. As a title factory, there is only one institution that can successfully compete with it, and that is the Masonic order with its thirty-three degrees and its list of officers, from Master to Most Potent Sovereign Grand Commander.

It is clear that, in order to do justice to our theme in the time allotted, we must confine our attention to the college proper, known at Harvard simply as the "College," at Yale as the "Academical Department"; at Illinois University as the "College of Literature and Science." Our problem is now very much simplified, and yet it is complex enough.

What is a college course? Let us imagine a young man, of average intelligence, trying to find an answer to this question. He has studied the common school branches until he can pass an examination for a second grade certificate, has been advised to take a college course, and wants to follow this good advice, as he ought to of, course. By some fortunate providence, he steers clear of the shoal of the business college, with its plausible motto, "Let your boys learn what they will practice when they are men," and of the so-called Normal School, which promises to teach him in three years more than the "old fogy colleges" can in six, and he sets sail for the deeper waters of a liberal education. He secures the catalogues of all the degree-conferring colleges of this State and begins his liberal education by studying them, to find out what a college course is. In doing so he makes a number of interesting discoveries, which I will briefly summarize.

The length of time required for him to complete a college course is very uncertain. To be sure, nearly all the colleges group the studies of their courses under four years: Freshman, Sophomore, Junior and Senior; but one college will admit him to the Freshman class with nearly one term's work to spare; in another course he is just ready to enter the Freshman class, and others require of him additional preparatory study, varying from two-thirds of a year to three years.

The Illinois colleges do not offer him the same courses and degrees; several give him "Hobson's choice" of one, while others permit him to choose from two, three, or even four literary courses. In the main, they confine themselves to the classical and scientific courses.

There are various scientific courses; viz: The Latin Scientific, the Greek Scientific, the English Scientific, and the Scientific. Some colleges promise to make him a Bachelor of Science on completion of the Scientific course; while others promise him the degree Bachelor of Philosophy, on completion of their Latin Scientific course, which is essentially the same. As a rule the scientific courses are shorter than the classical; they contain no Greek except in one case as an optional, and in another as a part of a Greek scientific course; they contain less Latin than the classical, in several cases none at all. All things considered, the scientific course is the most uncertain factor in our problem of determining what a college course is; and Dr. Gulliver might with truth repeat what he said some years ago, while President of Knox College: "The degree Bachelor of Science informs me that the possessor has studied no Greek and but little Latin, in short, that he does not know very much. I sometimes confer it, but always with profound pity for the recipient."

The Degree of Bachelor of Arts is a little better. All colleges whose catalogues I have examined bestow it. Here, at least, is a uniformity. There is at least one snake in this Ireland, but I fear it is about the only one.

The following table groups the twenty-nine colleges under consideration, according to the time required to secure the degree Bachelor of Arts, for a student who has passed a satisfactory examination in the common school branches, viz: arithmetic, grammar, reading, writing, spelling, United States history and geography.

I have thought best to give simply the number and not the names, of colleges in each group, but would most earnestly request the authorities of Illinois colleges to ascertain by a careful study of their classical and preparatory courses where their respective institutions fit in this table, and to most of them I would respectfully suggest the propriety of "coming up higher."

> Eight colleges outside of Illinois require about 7 years.
> Three colleges in Illinois require about 7 years.
> Three colleges in Illinois require from 6½ to 7 years.
> Five colleges in Illinois require from 6 to 6½ years.
> Nine colleges in Illinois require from 5 to 6 years.
> One college in Illinois requires about 4⅔ years.

Mr. President, ladies and gentlemen:—I am not inordinately proud of this showing made by Illinois colleges.

The lines of study pursued in the classical courses of our Illinois colleges are largely the same. Electives are introduced in some, but none have as yet come up, or down, to the level of Harvard, the oldest of American colleges.

A study of the requirements for admission and graduation enables us to make an inventory of the mental attainments of a Harvard Bachelor of Arts: He understands the English language and is slightly familiar with its literature; he has studied algebra through quadratics, and plane geometry; he has studied rhetoric and English composition, prepared essays on themes assigned and engaged in disputations; he has listened to one scientific lecture a week during the Freshman year, first on chemistry and then on physics; he can read easy prose German and French. This is all we know positively. In addition he can read easy prose in one ancient language, but we do not know whether it is Greek or Latin; he has passed an examination in history, it may be of Greece and Rome, or it may be of England and the United States; he has also been examined either in elementary astronomy or elementary physics. All his other studies have been chosen from a long list of electives. We are informed, however, that "students who prefer a course like that usually prescribed in colleges can easily secure it by a corresponding choice of studies"; and it is hardly necessary to add that students who prefer light work, can easily make their choice accordingly and save valuable time for base ball and boating.

I have said enough to show that there is a sad lack of uniformity in college courses, both as to the time required for them, and studies prescribed in them. Among the causes leading to this state of affairs are, probably, the increase of human knowledge, and the multiplication of denominational colleges.

As the sum total of human knowledge increases, the amount required for a liberal education naturally increases. The gentleman who preceded me on the programme kindly furnished me with a catalogue of Illinois College just fifty years old. At that time no natural science was required except physics, and no analytical geometry, no calculus and no modern languages. In physics the work must have been far less than now; for many new inventions and discoveries have been made since then, and a man can hardly be considered liberally educated unless he knows something of them. Yale started out with a college course of three years, and probably less was required for admission to it than now to the four years' course. The colleges of the country have been endeavoring to keep pace with their time; in this march some have fallen behind, others possibly have gone too far. The college course has been stretched and stretched, until it was found impossible to include everything in it; then electives were resorted to, or parallel courses laid down. Unfortunately, there has not been enough concert of action about this, and the result is as has been shown.

So, too, the multiplication of denominational colleges has had its effect. To a certain extent a new college draws on the patronage of the older ones, and weakens them; in so far as new patronage is created by planting a college in a new community, or under the care of a new denomination, it consists often of persons who have had very limited preparatory training and are of somewhat mature years; the new college is inadequately supplied with teachers, and yet desires to graduate classes as large as possible and as speedily as possible. All these causes combine to shorten the original classical course and to create still shorter courses in the new colleges, and unless the older ones follow their example the result again is a difference in college courses.

If these are the causes, what about the remedies? I would not, neither would you, I believe, remove either of these two causes, if you could, and what is more to the point, we could not if we would. The human mind, ever active, will continue to explore new fields of thought; the Newtons of our day, standing by the shore with the ocean of knowledge lying unexplored before them, will continue to pick up their pebbles of truth, and college courses will continue to embody, in part at least, the truths thus discovered.

So also, communities having no college will continue to offer inducements to secure one; benevolent Christians who see that the word of God is being crowded out of schools supported by popular taxation, will continue to offer their means to found Christian colleges, where the word may have free course; religious denominations will continue to take advantage of these offers and establish their first or their fiftieth college; young men and women living near these new colleges will be drawn into them and will desire "to go through college," and I, for one, am thankful that the opportunities for gaining a higher education are constantly becoming more abundant.

No! the causes of the diversity in college courses must not, can not be removed; but a remedy must be found or our degrees will become valueless. Already, as keen an observer as Leonard W. Bacon, D. D., declares that "A. B." is as meaningless an abbreviation as exists, with the exception of "D. D.," which latter combination, even Bismarck, the iron Chancellor, is now authorized to affix to his awe-inspiring name.

Permit me to suggest a few measures which this association, or section, might take, to produce some degree of uniformity in our courses.

1. The adoption of a resolution to be submitted to all the colleges of the State, recommending that their courses be brought to a uniform standard, as to the time required to prepare for, and complete them. It may be objected that this would abolish so-called shorter courses, and deprive many of the privilege of getting a college degree, who can now secure one. Granted; but thousands have been able to live usefully and die happy without owning a parchment diploma adorned with a blue-ribbon and stamped with a college seal, and, humiliating as the confession may be, we might as well admit that this is still possible. Besides, would it not be better that a hundred persons should obtain a degree that means, at least, a definite amount of literary work performed, than that two hundred should obtain one which has no ascertainable meaning?

2. I would suggest the appointment of a committee to prepare and submit to the colleges (*a*) a list of prescribed studies for admission to, and completion of their courses, these prescribed studies to occupy about two-thirds of the time allotted to

the courses; (*b*) a list of electives from which the remaining third of the work may be chosen, either by the college authorities as prescribed studies or by the students under the supervision of the Faculty as electives.

This plan, so far as carried out, would establish a standard of amount of work required for a degree; would also fix two-thirds of the studies to be pursued, and yet would have sufficient elasticity to accommodate itself to the varying needs and notions of the colleges in different communities.

3. I would suggest that the colleges having thus adopted a uniform standard of requirement for admission, as well as graduation, appoint a joint committee on accredited high schools and academies. The University of Illinois already has a list of high schools whose graduates can be admitted without examination. Would not the fact that an accredited high school could have its graduates admitted to a dozen, or twenty, colleges in the State, do much toward establishing that helpful relation between the colleges and secondary schools, which is so desirable?

As it is at present, we can not expect the high schools to do much toward preparing their students for college, simply because it is impossible for them to find out what preparation the colleges desire.

I have purposely confined myself mainly to Illinois colleges, because this association can hardly hope to influence directly the 300 or more colleges of the country. An effort has been made in the college section of the National Educational Association to bring some order out of the confusion now existing; but that body is too unwieldy, and too peripatetic, to accomplish much. Committees are appointed but do not get together; reports are read to be acted on at a subsequent meeting, but the subsequent meeting is several thousand miles away, and the report is lost "in transit."

The colleges of Illinois are near enough together to touch

elbows; members of committees from any part of the State can meet in Chicago, with comparatively little difficulty.

I, therefore, sincerely hope that this meeting will not adjourn without making an effort, at least, to secure uniform courses in the colleges of this State.

HOW CAN SCHOOL PROGRAMMES BE SHORTENED AND ENRICHED?

BY REV. HERBERT F. FISK, D. D., PROFESSOR OF PEDAGOGICS, NORTHWESTERN UNIVERSITY, EVANSTON, ILL.

"Can school programmes be shortened and enriched?" is the title of a paper read by President Eliot at Washington in February last, before the Department of Superintendence of the National Educational Association. This paper was published in the *Atlantic Monthly* of August.

The schools President Eliot has in mind are the public schools below the grade of the high school. If his premises are granted, his argument is conclusive.

First: It is of immense importance to the American people, that the age of American youths at the completion of their professional education should be lowered.

Secondly. The time occupied in their education may, conceivably, be shortened by shortening the post-graduate or professional course, by shortening the college course, by shortening the preparatory or high school course, or, lastly, by shortening the grammar school course.

But, the post-graduate course cannot be shortened; the college course cannot be materially shortened; the course of specific preparation for college—say of four years—as at Exeter Academy or at any well-conducted high school, cannot be shortened without loss (for, he says, "any secondary school taking its pupils in the average condition of the boys who enter Exeter Academy can hardly do more for them in four years than is now accomplished for them in that academy.)

It follows plainly, that what must be done at some point and cannot be done at any other stage in the pupil's progress, must be done in the grammar school course. And what must be done can be done. President Eliot then proceeds to indicate how it can be done.

With much that he says we find ourselves in sympathy, but we cannot sympathize with his tone of urgency and insistence, as if the lowering of the average age of admission to college from 19 years to 18 years, were a question of the highest possible importance. His anxiety on this point is expressed in a tone of alarm. "College men," he says, "are anxiously looking to see if the American school courses cannot be shortened, so that our boys may come to college at eighteen instead of nineteen;" and again, "the anxiety with which men charged with the conduct of college education look at this question, is increased by the relative decline of American colleges as a whole;" and again, he speaks of "*this serious difficulty*" which is embarrassing the whole course of American education."

In these utterances President Eliot speaks for himself and not for all—not for most—college men. He may be right. To his penetrating vision a real monster big with evil omen may loom threateningly, while men less discerning have failed to see it in all its fateful and portentous proportions; or is he a conjurer and does he impose upon himself with his own magic? [He certainly deceives himself in thinking that he is warranted in speaking thus for college men as a body. At a meeting of college officers of the New England colleges, held more than a year ago, the majority of the college men present declared themselves not anxious that the average age of admission to college should be materially reduced.]

Many are disposed to think that certain advantages are gained from life and study in college by students who graduate at 23 years of age and upwards which are not in equal degree secured by younger students. These young men coming to their studies of history and philosophy, of ethics and politics, and to their participation in those business affairs of class and fraternity organizations, and in those literary and oratorical competitions which make college life a little world, get a degree of discipline from these studies and activities, a thoroughness of preparation for their larger spheres of action in the world of business and politics, which at an earlier age they could not gain.

It is not altogether certain that President Eliot is right in thinking that any *balance* of advantage lies in favor of the earlier graduation. It is quite certain that the advantages in favor of early graduation are not so surely known and so tremendously big that the *burning* educational question of the day is how to get our boys into college a year earlier than now. One reason named by President Eliot for his own anxiety and the alleged anxiety of college men with reference to the age of admission to college is "the relative decline of American colleges as a whole," and in proof of this relative decline he states that from 1875 to 1884 there was an increase of only 23 per cent. in the number of students in colleges, while the population is thought to have increased about 33 per cent. We ought not to lose sight of the fact that our increase of population, both by immigration and propagation, belongs in much the largest part to those classes whose traditions and inheritance practically bar the way for themselves and for their children to a liberal education. An advance of 23 per cent. in the number of college students may be considered in good reason not a relative decline but a substantial advance. The colleges are more than holding their own in their influence with the distinctly American population, and in their power to attract and hold students.

Mr. Eliot laments that "for sixty years the average age of admission to Harvard College has been rising, and has now reached the extravagant limit of eighteen years and ten months."

He does not tell us, what is essential to a just consideration of this alarming fact, that Harvard College has been advancing its requirements for admission quite beyond the increase of age which he deplores. Dr. Peabody, the venerable college pastor at Cambridge for many years, and still connected with the faculty of Harvard College, said at a meeting of the National Educational Association a few years ago, that Harvard College requires now a better education for admission, than forty years ago it required for graduation. But Mr Eliot would not for a moment entertain the thought of lowering the present conditions of admission. He expresses his solicitude that "the standard of the A. B. may not be lowered," but "that our boys may come to college at eighteen instead of nineteen, and that they may bring to college at eighteen more than they now bring at nineteen." Yet, though we are inclined to smile at President Eliot's distress over the "extravagant limit now reached for the average age of admission to Harvard College, and over the mournful fact that the average college student in the smaller colleges is undoubtedly nearly twenty-three years old at graduation," he may have some wise counsel for us that we shall welcome with cordial appreciation.

If there is no such urgent need that our school courses should be *shortened*, we shall be very glad to find that they can be enriched. If they can be both shortened and enriched, we shall be quite willing to gain time as well as'enrichment. Indeed, the very process of shortening is an *enrichment* provided in the condensing process everything essential be retained. The engine that can make the longest run in the shortest time with the heaviest load is of largest value. The training of the mind that gives equally good results in a shorter time, not only saves time for other uses, but produces richer results in the mind itself, making it by so much the more perfect instrument of the human will.

The time saved may be used, if it should amount to a full

year in some cases, or to two years possibly, in other cases, in giving to these exceptional pupils an earlier entrance on a college course; or it may be made to enrich the student by his use of it in manual training, in studies and readings parallel to his class work and broadening the range of his thought, in elementary studies supplementary to his school course and anticipating the advanced studies that are to come years later, in collecting cabinets of geology and natural history specimens, or in gaining familiarity with some chosen authors in the literature of our native tongue.

To complete his answer to the question, "Can school programmes be shortened and enriched?" Mr. Eliot was obliged to justify his affirmation by showing how the desired result could be reached.

First. He would have better teachers employed; and in order to do this, "all friends of public education should constantly strive to have a better tenure of office established,—a tenure during good behavior and efficiency." "Consideration, dignity and quietness of mind go with a permanent tenure."

He would also "increase the average skill of teachers by raising the present low proportion of male teachers," alleging "the superiority of men as teachers," not on the ground of superior intelligence or faithfulness, but for the reason that "men or women who take up the service of teaching as a temporary expedient are unsatisfactory material," and women, oftener than men, "enter the service of the public schools without intention of long following the business, and that women are absent from duty two to three times as much as men; so that the larger the proportion of women in any system of public schools, the larger will be the percentage of newly appointed teachers every year, and the larger the amount of work done by temporary substitutes." He would also secure better teachers by urging superintendents and committees and all wise lovers of the public schools to advocate the liberal expenditure of money for teaching rather than for mechanical appliances or buildings. "Cheap teachers and expensive apparatus are the reverse of wise practice."

Secondly. He would have better programmes. "The courses" —he takes those of the city of Boston as representing the average American programmes—"are not substantial enough, not enough meat in the diet, do not bring forward the child fast enough to maintain his interest." To the objection that there is complaint now of overpressure, he answers that this comes not of work, but from lack of interest; that "one problem a child cannot solve wears more than ten which he can; that American teaching in all grades of schools and in colleges has been chiefly driving and judging, while it ought to be leading and inspiring."

Thirdly. He would save time by diminishing the time spent in reviews, and by fewer examinations, and by being content without the accuracy of knowledge and statement often demanded.

Fourthly. He disfavors the irregular promotion of brighter children and favors the regular promotion of the great body of children at the ages set down on the programme, and advises that the examinations be made light enough to insure this result.

Fifthly. He favors longer hours in school, and the provision of vacation schools for the least favored children.

Not all of this counsel can we accept as equally wise. Some of it we shall after scrutiny reject as unsound. Most of it, it will be well for us, the teachers of Illinois, to accept, and, as we have opportunity, to apply.

We repeat, that we cannot excite in our own mind the agitation that worries Mr. Eliot over what he conceives to be the "relative decline of the colleges." Still, we shall agree with him that the colleges of Illinois and of other states would like to see and could well care for many more students from the homes of Illinois than are now persuaded to seek a liberal education; and that great advantage would accrue to the State of Illinois, if every year there were added to the number of college alumni in her population five times as many new graduates as at present, trained men to be leaders of men and organizers of labor in all professions, and in all mercantile and industrial pursuits. The number of those who will seek a liberal education will be increased by any improvement in the thoroughness and real value of the training in the elementary schools. A boy's relish or distaste for learning which really decides him for or against his prosecution of a liberal education is often determined by the influence of his earliest teachers.

The securing of better trained, more devoted, more efficient teachers in the public schools will send out of these schools into the colleges more pupils and those pupils better prepared. To give capable and experienced teachers a more liberal compensation and a securer tenure of office, will bring into the service of the state a larger proportion of men, and will secure and retain in service a larger number of both men and women of eminent ability and superior professional skill. This result secured, the school programmes will be enriched, and the overflow of riches will beautify and gladden the entire state. The benefits of education are like mercy, their "quality is not strained." They bless him that gives and him that takes, and then they cease not in their beneficence, but each one who receives a benefit becomes himself a benefactor and in ever widening circles the initial impulse of blessing propagates itself until there is not a hamlet but is made richer, not an acre of soil but has added value, not a weary toiler but bears his burdens more easily.

In Mr. Eliot's first point we confess our indebtedness to him for good counsel. Not that he has said anything new or strange, but that what he says is true, that it is worth saying, and worth repeating, and that repetition of it is likely to deepen conviction of its truth with our legislators and our boards of education, on whose liberality we are dependent for the increased compensation which is needed to secure the better teachers.

2. Mr. Eliot's second and most important counsel will perhaps be conceded by all to be true when stated in its general form, that the programmes can be bettered. We are all of us willing to acknowledge in general the imperfection of our work, though prone to deny, sometimes promptly and with spirit, any specific imperfections alleged by our critics. We adopt the language of the litany : "Have mercy upon us poor miserable sinners," but will have it that in this or that particular, in which others see us to have been wrong, we were just right.

When Mr. Eliot says "the diet is not substantial enough," I imagine many will be quick to claim that in this point he is all wrong. But is he not *right?* Is he not VERY RIGHT? Is not this the truest and most vital criticism of the American schools of to-day, that "the programmes are not substantial enough," that they "do not bring the child forward fast enough to maintain interest and induce him to put forth his strength." Has not the public school system below the high school gradually come to take its present shape from the anxiety of teachers and superintendents to make it practicable for *all* the children in the community, the most sluggish in intellect, the weakest in physical endurance, the least favored in home conditions, to keep pace with the yearly progress of the school work? As a result, the work for all has been graded down to the infirmity of the weakest, while those of medium or superior capacity have been able to meet the requirements of the school course while putting one-half or one-third of their time and strength into their studies. Hence, idleness and mischief in the school-room taxing the invention of the teacher to restrain the bright boy by penalties, when a wise course would be to seek to incite him to high ambition and noble enthusiasm, guiding him in special studies and rewarding, with special honors, worthy efforts and noteworthy attainments. Hence, perplexity of parents to keep the boy, idle and restless and mischievous at school, from being discontented with profitable uses of his time at home. Hence, out of our best schools, and among the children of cultivated homes, boys of ten or twelve years on the streets out of school hours, day and evening,—not habituated at any hour of the day to hard tasks in study—all their school life and all their home life self-indulgent, ease-loving, pleasure-loving, mischief-loving,—poisoning their bodies with cigarettes, and poisoning their minds with the reading of trashy or filthy novels. Is this a picture of the imagination? Would it were so! But does not the knowledge of every citizen summon before him, if not in his own children, in some children of his neighbors, a vision of that which is, alas, too real? But it will be said in exculpation of the schools and officers, "Have parents no responsibility? Is not the child out of school hours beyond the jurisdiction of the teacher, and if the child's idle and vicious habits give little hope of stability of character and usefulness, is the teacher to take the blame to himself, when he labors with unceasing solicitude for the intellectual and moral welfare of his pupils?"

Let us, friends and fellow teachers, be willing to see the whole truth as to our responsibility. The teacher's responsibility does not end with the closing of the school for the day or for the term. No more does the parent's responsibility cease for the day when the pupil enters the school room, to be resumed by him when the pupil passes out from the presence of the teacher. The partnership of teacher and parent, in the shaping of the child's future by intellectual and moral training, is like the partnership of father and mother in the physical endowment of the child and in parental care, an undivided and indivisible partnership. "The whole child is sent to school." Body, mind and heart are committed to the teacher. An eminent educator in an eastern school said to me, "It matters not what my teacher of arithmetic is, in habits or belief, so that he knows arithmetic and can teach arithmetic." No falser, no more pernicious doctrine than this. Let us away with it, if it has found lodgment in our pedagogic creed. Let us be intolerant of it wherever it finds expression. The teacher imparts himself, his whole self, to the pupil. The teacher's responsibility toward the pupil is discharged only when he has done his utmost for the pupil's good in all respects, and he should not be satisfied that he has done his utmost for the pupil's good, if that pupil in any hour of the twenty-four or in any day of the seven, goes wrong. Just as a mother, who has enshrined herself in her boy's heart in the years of his childhood, when that boy is separated from her by years of wandering over all oceans and continents, should be with him in his thought of her a restraining and guiding and impelling power to hold him to purity and honor, so the teacher's well-devised programme of work and right personal example and firm exercise of authority and unfailing sympathetic interest in all that concerns the boy's welfare, having given wise direction to his energies in the hours of his school days, should give character to the boy's actions in all other hours, putting the teacher at the boy's side, a genial presence, in his work and in his play, in his solitude and among his boon companions, in his day dreams and in his dreams by night, making him to recoil, when tempted, from those thoughts and actions which he would be ashamed to entertain or to commit if the friendly eye of the teacher were upon him. Is this too much for the teacher to exact of himself? This is the ideal, and short of it we should never rest satisfied. There is a principal of a high school of 800 pupils in a New England city of 100,000 population, who has achieved a success most of us would have thought impossible. Before two months have passed at the beginning of the year he can call by name every one of the pupils of the newly-entered class, and he has made every one of them feel that he has an interest in whatever concerns their studies, their health, their plans, their pleasures. He meets this lowest class two hours each week for a year,

When I look at the programme, I see that in the second year multiplication and division tables to 12's are completed. From this point, for five years, more than two-thirds of the time on arithmetic is wasted. Better results in arithmetic would be secured by spending fifteen minutes a day for three years in drill in rapid combinations, and in extending the multiplication table to 25, then resuming the arithmetic and proceeding with accuracy, and rapidity, and pleasure to the pupil, scarcely ever known by pupils under the present programmes. And in the last two years of the grammar school some time could be found to alternate lessons in arithmetic with lessons in geometry and physics.

The time thus saved might judiciously be used in reading wholesome biographies adapted to the advancing age of pupils, giving early a taste for literature and a love of history, and making it possible for teachers to vary the amount of reading suggested to pupils according to their home conditions of leisure or occupation, and according to the facility developed in taking the sense of what is read.

Not too much time is given to geography, but in this time much more can be done than is usually done in suggesting collateral reading, making the text book lesson the starting point for wide excursions in literary reading on topics suggested by the names of historic places and persons named in the text book. Such reading would have its great value, not only as giving occupation for the pupil's leisure time at home, and filling up all time in school, to the cure of mischievous propensities, and not only in filling the mind with information at a time when memory is most impressible and retentive, to be of untold value in after years, but in disciplining the pupil's mind to the ready interpretation of thought and to the power of free and animated expression. This would make it possible to save much of the three years now spent on formal English grammar, which could profitably be given to the study of the elements of some kindred language, the French or German or Latin. The French programmes, as recited by Mr. Eliot, in these respects have excellent features for our imitation·

They give not more than one-third the time we do to arithmetic. They give to the French language and literature much more time than we to English, and yet at eight years of age the French boy is set to studying some foreign language, either the German or English, and, by this daily study of his own language in comparison with another, he comes to understand it better than if it were studied apart by itself for many years. The French boy's study of history begins with biography, as we have suggested should be the case with the American child.

We conclude that Mr. Eliot is right in claiming that the American programmes can be improved, enriched, very much enriched. Meanwhile the intelligent American teacher, overcoming the inertia that contents him with keeping up to the system, and devising ways of his own to quicken the pace of his pupils in what he is required to have them do, so as to secure time for what they will take delight in, for recreations outside of the curriculum, may win credit to himself—to herself—from pupils and parents, and have the satisfaction of seeing an unprecedented development of intelligence and moral earnestness in the hearts and minds of many pupils. Many teachers have gone a little way in this direction. Who will have the courage of conviction and the pioneering sagacity to blaze the way through this, as yet, untracked forest, making a new path in which others may follow?

Mr. Eliot, in his third point, proposing to save time by less reviewing and by fewer examinations, and by making no strenuous claim upon the pupils for accuracy of knowledge and accuracy of statement, is wholly wrong as he has been in the first and second points wholly right. No time is more profitably spent than in judicious reviews, which should always be *new* views, a reconsideration of subjects in new combinations, and in the guiding light of new inquiries. No more valuable educational implement is there than a judiciously-conducted examination, and these should be frequent—tests not so much of what students remember as of what they can do, confining memory to the fewest elementary matters, the essential data of reasoning and leading them not to recall by memory but to reproduce by reasoning processes, the rules and formulas in the mathematics and in the languages. And as to accuracy of attainment—accuracy in the essential elements of any topic, accuracy in the process of reasoning, accuracy in statement of results, if the pupil is ever to be trustworthy as a servant or as a master of other men, he must from the first be taught to be accurate. Strange counsel to teachers from a teacher of teachers, from the President of the oldest college in the country, that they are not to expect to bring on their pupils to the habit of accuracy in adding long columns of figures, or to the ability to find the greatest common divisor or the least common multiple of several numbers. Let us hope few teachers will be misled by these unwise counsels.

4. In his fourth point he is partly right and partly wrong—right in deprecating the common evil of retardation, wrong in disfavoring irregular promotions. The system is slow enough so that few children, unless interrupted by absence, should be allowed to fall behind. And this evil should be prevented, not by grading down the examinations to reach the infirmity of dullness, but by enkindling the zeal and aiding the halting steps of the naturally sluggish children so as to bring them up to the requirements of judicious examinations.

The irregular promotion of strong pupils is just the thing wanted to serve their interests and to quicken the pulse of the whole system of schools and keep the blood from stagnating. Where pupils are entered in school at the age of 8 or 9, as not unfrequently happens, it should be expected that they would advance more rapidly than those who enter at 5 or 6, and would do in one year the work of two or three. So, when the child's heredity and home environment give him exceptional advantage, he should be encouraged within the limits of prudent regard for health, and with the concurrence of his parents, to proceed ahead of his class and overtake the class in advance, and many pupils can save two and some three years, and do the whole work well.

It is just this fault of the systems now in vogue, holding classes to regular solid advancement year by year, and saying to teachers, "within this year [the fourth year of the course,] give exercises in addition, subtraction, multiplication, and division; multiplier 3 figures, divisor 12 or less, result in no case to exceed three periods," that gives occasion for many educators to say—better the old unsystematic schools of a generation ago than these restraining bands that hold back a wide-awake pupil who can easily be led to move on beyond the prescribed routine, but no, "in no case for this year shall the sum exceed three periods."

The teacher in the handling of an improved programme should be free to exercise a wide discretion in modifying the programme. In the exercise of this freedom, under responsibility to superiors and to the public, he should be guided by such judgments as these:

The system is for the good of the individuals, not the individuals subordinate to the system.

The supreme interest of the teacher should be in the pupil— not in the school, not in his own reputation, not in the subjects he teaches, but in the pupil. The life is more than meat, the soul is more than truth. The great Teacher valued the Truth he came to teach as a means to an end, praying for his disciples, the pupils whom he yearned over with a longing which makes him in this, as in other respects, the great exemplar for all true teachers, "Sanctify them through thy truth." "All effective Christian work for men," says Dr. Smyth in the *Andover Review*, "requires an open eye for the individual, a love for persons." In the same spirit we may say, all educational work worthy to be esteemed highly successful, requires an open eye for the individual, a love of the teacher for his pupils, one by one—a love that reckons upon their differences, and adapts itself in teaching methods and in arts of inspiration and guidance to each, as food should be prepared differently for different ages and tastes, and as an overgrown and awkward boy should not have his clothing determined by his years, but fitted to his person.

Discipline is worth more than knowledge. The tests determining promotions should be tasks given to be done, rather than tests of memory. These tests should seek to ascertain, not so much the amount of present knowledge, as the power to learn, to interpret, to give expression to thought. The faculty of Princeton College made a mistake when they refused to receive Alexander Hamilton's application for admission with the privilege of advancing as rapidly as he could, doing the college work thoroughly. He gained admission to King's College (now Columbia College) on his own terms, and made the course in two years. The Hamiltons are few in number, but they should have their chance. All our schools should be elastic enough in their requirements to give natural powers, original genius, in the individual teacher and in the individual pupil, a free chance for activity and for coming to their best.

Finally, the tasks assigned, the tests applied, the rewards given, whether words of commendation, premiums, or figures in a record book, must be so wisely devised that the pupils of highest ability shall not too easily be satisfied, and the feeblest pupils may not too easily be discouraged.

LIMITATION OF STATE PROVISION FOR EDUCATION.

BY REV. J. B. MCMICHAEL, D. D., PRESIDENT OF MONMOUTH COLLEGE, MONMOUTH, ILL.

Every truth has its limitations. Pushed beyond the boundaries which circumscribe its field of action, it becomes an error. It is out of right relations with the established order of things and is a disturber of the peace in the field which it enters. That I have a right to do as I please is the magna charta of personal liberty, but, unlimited, it is destructive of the liberty of everyone else. When I interfere with the rights of another, my unlimited liberty ceases to be a rule of right action. It is the limitation which makes it right.

Institutions which enjoy the right to exist are subject to like limitations and can only enjoy the right to exist as long as these limitations are respected. When transcended, injury is done to all, their efficiency is impaired and the end for which they were established is defeated.

The family, the church, and the state are three institutions organized to meet the wants and secure the civil, social and religious rights of man. He is a three-fold being and these institutions are founded in his nature and are necessary to his symmetrical development. To realize his possibilities the same individual must be a member of the three. This may be questioned by those who are tenacious for everything else but the development of their spiritual natures; but it will not be questioned by anyone who has a proper appreciation of what he is and what he was intended to be. Wherever else it might be necessary to elaborate this point it is certainly not necessary in the presence of men who would sooner question the reality of their social and civil relations than to doubt their spiritual. By all such, the family, the church, and the state are recognized as institutions which have a right to exist, and, as for the others, it will be time enough to attend to them when they shall have succeeded in eliminating the moral element of manhood.

Each of these institutions is sovereign in its domain, servant outside of it. Inside it commands, outside it obeys. Thus far and no farther. The state cannot do the work of the church nor can the church do the work of the state; and when they attempt it the work of neither will be done. To do its own work each must have its own agencies, educate its own subjects and attend strictly to its own business. There is room for both of them, occupying the same territory and claiming allegiance from the same subjects. While there is to be no union of the church and state, there is to be no conflict between them. Under God each is to contribute to the welfare of the other. "Render unto Cæsar the things which are Cæsar's, and unto God the things that are God's."

The protestant church has ever been the fast and unswerving friend of the public school system. Were it not for the Christian element of the country our schools would not be in the healthy condition they now are. Far from it. What would they be without the active support of the protestant church? In view of this, should the church raise the question of limitation of state appropriation for school purposes, it is neither in accordance with the facts nor in sympathy with the spirit of fairness that she should be represented as unfriendly to state schools; and to whatever extent I may here represent the views of the church on this question, I must not be so understood. On the contrary, we maintain that popular government is conditioned upon popular education, and that the republic, under forfeit of her right to live, is bound to see to it that such an education is provided.

Of necessity, there must be schools operated by the state and for the state. These schools are not to be limited to the primary or rudimentary schools, not even to the high schools, provided they do not put on university airs, undertaking to give instruction in the whole range of literatures, arts, sciences and philosophies, and rounding up with a graduation which suggests that there is nothing beyond to be desired. Nor will we object to the state normal if it is to be what it professes to be, a professional school for training teachers. But you can't train until you have something to train. Education is first in order, and it should be obtained at those schools which the state has already founded to give it. We object to the state making another appropriation to educate the same persons for whom appropriations are made to the high school, the grammar school and possibly to the kindergarten. Eliminating these, those who remain will be better taught and at a reduced cost to the state; and, in addition to this, the people will have the satisfaction of knowing that their money is expended in accordance with the terms of assessment, the training of teachers. Nor do we approach the state university in an iconoclastic spirit, but rather to set bounds to its ambition in the direction of the state treasury. Even these it is our purpose to place along the lines of justice and equity. Like conditions call for like appropriations, but as the conditions in the various states and at various times in the same state are seldom if ever the same, no estimate in dollars and cents can be fixed upon as the rule of equity in every case, but each case at the time is to be determined upon its own merit.

Were there no institutions excepting the state to be taken into consideration in passing upon educational appropriations, still, upon other grounds of a sound political economy, limitations must be observed, not so restricted, it is true, but they must nevertheless obtain. But the state is not the only institution founded in the interest of man, and it is therefore not to assume the right to lay under tribute all his resources in the development of the state. The old Spartan idea that the state is everything and the man nothing but a citizen, a mere peg in the machinery of government, is not the idea of statehood and manhood to-day. We want something more than citizens—we want men. Good citizens are made out of good men, and you can't make them out of anything else.

1. I insist upon limited provision for education by the state because unlimited state instruction is dangerous in its tendencies, threatening not only the integrity of the federal constitution but the constitution of manhood. A bill recently introduced into the Senate of the United States by Senator Ingalls, and which is still pending, provides for the founding of a "great commanding national university, whose degrees, conferred only upon rigid examination, would become the standard by which literary and scientific eminence would be measured throughout the nation. Such a University, if successful, would become the seat of supreme academic influence, giving character to the curriculum, standard and aims of all state, local, and independent universities in the land." The logical outcome of such a scheme, should it be successfully inaugurated, would be the absolute centralization of a national system of education under government control. The realization of the national system includes the school in every neighborhood, the high school in every town, a higher one in every county, the normal in every congressional district, the university in every state, and all unified, and practically governed, by the university of the nation. Teachers, books, and methods, in every school within the system, are to be measured, fitted, and worn according to the pattern given from the central office. And in this system, and through these schools, everything, ranging through the whole diameter and around the entire circumference of human knowledge, is to be taught, excepting the knowledge of God. All this upon the

simple plea of citizenship. It may make citizens, but it will not make men. They have all been run through the same mould, fashioned after the same pattern, and polished by the same process, and is it illogical to conclude that the individuality and independence of manhood have been educated out of them, and they no longer think as men, made in the image of God, but as citizens, made in the image of the state and by the state? As big a thing as is the proposed national scheme of secular education, it is not as big as manhood, which it proposes to educate, and therefore under the instruction of such a system the man must necessarily come infinitely short of his possibilities. Much might be said in behalf of the reserved rights of the states in educational matters, and of the unconstitutionality of the assumption and exercise of such powers by the government, but it shall not be said here. I am content to say that such unlimited state provision for schools is a violation of the constitution of manhood.

2. I also object, beyond limited restrictions, to state appropriations for the higher education, because it unjustly discriminates against the church. The discrimination is not in the fact that the state makes no appropriation to the church for the education of her subjects. She wants none. She voluntarily builds and operates her own schools in addition to what has been collected from her membership to support the higher education of the state. When her membership, as citizens, pay their full proportion of the school fund for the education of the people, is it not a stinging injustice that they should still be taxed for university education, the education of lawyers, physicians, and professional experts, for the good of the common people; and as a compensation for this, is granted the privilege of founding and operating her own academies, colleges, and universities for the higher education of the church. It is not difficult for Americans to see that a state church is a costly luxury to dissenting Christians. Against it our fathers protested to the extent of expatriation,

and to this day their children are delicately sensitive upon the subject. Is not the principle of the establishment here? There all must pay to the support of the establishment. Should any through conscientious convictions dissent from its teachings and withdraw from its fellowship, they are graciously accorded the privilege of building their own meeting house, paying their own preacher, and the preacher of the establishment as well.

Beyond certain limitations, taxation to support higher education ceases to be a virtue. By her schools the church is educating the people of the state, and the education which is good for the church is good for the state. Over one hundred voluntary schools, academies, seminaries, colleges and universities have been chartered by the state of Illinois which do not receive from her a dollar for their support. After educating nine out of every ten who receive more than a high school education, she is then equally taxed with the other citizens of the commonwealth to educate the other *one*. It seems to me that the line of limitation to state provision should be found somewhere in this latitude, sometimes above, sometimes below the peaks along the high school range, according to the relative condition of church and state.

3. Again, I insist upon the limitation of appropriation on the ground of the character of state schools. It is readily conceded that many devoted Christian men are to be found in these institutions whose life and teaching are a positive force in the line of Christian manhood; but, on the other hand, consider the number whose life and teaching are positively in the other direction, and the institution, as an institution, confessedly stands at zero upon the subject of Christian theism.

"The tide," says President Porter, "is now setting strongly towards the complete secularization of our public educational system. It may be the current will prevail. Should it rush through our higher schools, and sweep out from them all opportunity for reflective thought on God, and duty, and immortality;

should it exclude all study of history in the light of God's presence and guiding hand, and all inspiration of literature which is furnished by faith and worship—it will give us an education so barren and degrading that Christian parents will abandon the high schools in abhorrence, and will shun the universities to which they open the way as they would the infected wards of a house of death."

The question which concerns us here is not so much whether the state university is, should, or can be religious in its instruction, as whether it is or can be neutral upon the subject of religion. In fact, the question is, what kind of a religious philosophy is the state university to teach? Theistic or atheistic? The trend of the teaching of the school must teach something on the subject. How many of the subjects within the range of university instruction have not touched upon the supernatural in their origin and history? Certainly not the literatures, sciences and philosophies. They are woven in and out and through and through with mythical legends, lays and tales; with religions false and religion true. We might have a little empirical philosophy, cold logic and pure mathematics, but these might be had without the expensive luxury of a university. The studies pursued in the lower grade of schools are not so fraught with the great philosophical questions which pre-emenently belong to the university; and successfully to steer clear of God when following up these great philosophical lines of thought from the efficient to the final, or from the final to the efficient cause, is an attainment which human ingenuity has not yet reached. We quote from the Princeton *Review*, volume 2, page 133: "The universe must be conceived of either in a theistic or an atheistic light. It must originate in and develop through intelligence or in atoms and force and chance. Teleology must be acknowledged everywhere or denied everywhere. Philosophy, ethics, jurisprudence, political and social science can be conceived of and treated only from a theistic or from an atheistic point of view. The proposal to treat it from a neutral point of view is ignorant and absurd. .... It is certain that throughout the entire range of the higher education a position of religious indifferentism is an absolute impossibility, that along the entire line the relation of man and of the universe to the ever-present God and the supreme Lord of the conscience and heart, the non-affirmation of the truth is entirely equivalent to the affirmation at every point, of its opposite." Such schools do not provide such an education as the church requires, and therefore she must educate her own children, if that is the best the state can do for the higher education. She asks no division of the public funds for this purpose. She only asks that she be not robbed of her resources by taxation and compelled to support an atheistic institution that robs her hearth-stones and her altars of her sons and daughters and fits them for anything else than for citizenship in the kingdom of God.

4. I insist upon limitations of state provision for education because much of the education by the state is unnecessary.

(a) Much of the work done by the state university is in the line of special training, which neither directly nor indirectly is of any special advantage to the state; that is, those who have been so educated are of no greater advantage to the state than those who have been educated in other schools. Is it necessary that the people should be taxed for the education of lawyers, physicians, and experts in the various lines of the applied sciences? Luxuries are not necessaries. It is not equity that the many should be taxed for the luxuries of the few. When the people have paid for the professional education of their lawyers and doctors, they find that their services are no better and their bills no smaller than those who paid for their own education. The beneficiaries of the national academies at West Point and Annapolis are required to render some special service for value received, but the beneficiaries of our state schools are under no

LIMITATION OF STATE PROVISION FOR EDUCATION. 59

such obligations and recognize none. If a poor family, decimated by sickness and death, is unable to pay the doctor-bill, the state, which has educated the officiating doctor, must pay it herself. Ministers of the gospel, whom she does not educate, and who may be as beneficial in conserving the interest of the state, do not collect their bills in that way.

(b) It is unnecessary, because much of the instruction for which state appropriations are made can be given, will be given, and is being given by other schools founded and sustained by voluntary contributions. How many states are there in which there are not voluntary institutions which rival, if not surpass, the state university in the same state? Looking back toward the East, they are not the institutions which stand out most prominently. In many of the states you would scarcely know there was such an institution were it not for the annual racket in the legislature over the state appropriation. In some of the western and northwestern states such institutions are relatively more prominent. While building up their voluntary schools the people have been taxed to found and operate the state university, so that the race for preëminence has been an unequal one. But already, when looking over into the territories of some of these states, the university is not by any means the first object of educational interest that meets the eye.

In view of these facts we can safely leave the higher education in the hands of the munificent private patronage, which has, even in the childhood of our country, founded and supported Yale, Harvard, Princeton, Cornell, Johns Hopkins, and others of equal efficiency, if not of equal renown. And certainly against the most of these the terrible charge of sectarianism cannot be sustained. Their spirit is liberal enough for the most liberal government. It is wise for any government to stimulate and encourage such a spirit of patronage in behalf of the higher education.

If so much has already been done, more may be expected when greater private fortunes shall have been accumulated.

In May next, in honor of his son, who, had he lived, would then have been twenty-one years of age, Senator Stanford, of California, proposes to found a university on the Pacific coast at a cost of $20,000,000 in money and 76,000 acres of land for a campus. With such an institution in California surely the plea of necessity can not be urged in behalf of a state university in that state, at least. The like has already occurred in other states, and will continue to occur in others still with the encouragement of great opportunities, created by the limitation of state provision for education.

EDUCATION.

BY REV. WILLIAM C. ROBERTS, D. D., LL. D., PRESIDENT OF LAKE FOREST UNIVERSITY, ILLINOIS.

The necessity and value of general education have long since ceased to be matters of discussion. Even those who sympathize with Adam Smith in his opposition to governmental interference in higher and liberal education readily concede that that of the masses is an exception to this principle. It is generally believed that the better instructed the citizen is the more prosperous and influential will the state be. But before the benefits of general training and intelligence can be secured for the lower classes, the government, says Mr. Say, "must undertake it at public expense. It must establish primary schools for reading, writing and arithmetic, for they form the ground-work of knowledge and the sole means that can be secured at present for the civilization of the multitude. A nation cannot be said to be civilized nor, consequently, possessed of all the benefits of civilization until the people at large are versed in the elementary branches of knowledge."

It has been affirmed by many within fifteen years that the state should only supplement individual efforts in the direction of education, allowing all who are able to educate their children in schools supported by themselves, and confine its own efforts to the instruction of the poor. It was seen, however, that in such a plan there could be no system; the two kinds of schools would be antagonistic, and destitute of a common life, and the state would be unable to prevent the inculcation of principles that might prove subversive of its influence and authority. A general conviction was soon felt that education was too great an interest, and too closely connected with the commonwealth, to be left wholly without responsibility to the government. Then the homogeneousness of the nation was thought to be largely dependent on a general system of education. It was necessary it should be *general* in order to avoid invidious comparisons between the different classes of youth in the community. Hence the policy was finally adopted by every state in the Union of recognizing no distinction between the children of the rich and those of the poor, of putting them all on the same footing, and of treating them exactly alike.

Accepting the common school system as moderately wise and indispensably necessary to the welfare of the state, I call attention, for a few minutes, to the general theme of *Education*. This is one of the greatest questions of our day. It is becoming increasingly important every year. A limited class of scientific men and skeptics allege that there is nothing permanent in our present system of education. Rousseau declares that "that of the past, with the civilization based upon it, has been absolutely wrong," and offers as his advice to take the road directly opposite to that in which we have been traveling, promising that we shall thereby do right. Pestalozzi tells us that "he turned the car of European progress quite round," implying, of course, that it was moving in the wrong direction before he reversed its wheels. Herbert Spencer affirms "that we stand on the border land of a great discovery in education." Others of kindred spirit appear to be waiting in eager expectation for a total overthrow of our present system of education, and for the introduction of another based on a different principle. None of these foretellers of change, however, have ventured as yet to give us the outlines of their long-looked-for system of education.

Is there ground for these mysterious forebodings? Do the signs of the times point clearly in that direction? I answer, no. A strong presumptive argument against it is found in the fact that the main features of the present system of education have stood the tests of time. Education is not like the different species of superstition and false religious believed in and perpetuated by a single nation, but it is the production of the combined scholarship of the world. "I am sure," says President Payne, "that I do not overstate the fact when I say that the best thinkers through all past centuries have been devoted directly or indirectly to the problem of education and there is not a single phase of this problem which has not been subjected to the most rigid test of experience." Is it credible that such a vast and important interest as that of education should have been misunderstood by the acute philosophers of Greece, the practical statesmen of Rome and the learned of every nation since?

A second argument against the predicted revolution is found in the permanent character of the mind and the body — the objects to be trained. No essential change has taken place in these since the philosophers of Greece succeeded in developing both to as high a pitch of perfection as they can be. Are there in the mind buried treasures or undiscovered continents to be wrought upon by principles of education which are yet undiscovered? We have no evidence of this.

A third argument against the predicted change in education is that it would be out of analogy with similar interests that have come down to us through the ages. There can be no doubt that great progress has been made within a hundred years in the cause of education. "But progress," says another, "is not a force that acts spasmodically, but a logical and graduated evolution, in which the idea of to day is connected with that of yesterday as the latter is to a more remote past." A number of the elements of education have come down to us from remote antiquity. They have been modified to suit the circumstances of different nations, and not supplanted or set aside. There is no reason for believing that they will be wholly supplanted in the future.

Conservatism in education, as well as in religion, is of great value. It is the part of wisdom to act on the assumption that certain things are settled, and not to be examining their fundamental principles whenever science or the march of progress suggests a conflict between them and new theories. It is our duty to seek new improvements in the application of principles, and in extending and coördinating old lines of thinking and working. Each year should add something new to our system of education, either in doctrine or in practice; each day should bring out some revelation of truth, and all should be in the line of development and growth, rather than in the way of destruction and substitution!

I call your attention, secondly, to the *theories* respecting the *nature* of education. These are very many, but I can only refer to two or three. In the introduction to his Grammaire, Condillac claims that knowledge in the child is a simple product of experience, like the knowledge of the race. Herbert Spencer avers "that the child must accord both in mode and arrangement with the education of mankind as considered historically." The principles of education enunciated by Pestalozzi are the corollaries of those of Condillac and Spencer. The correctness of these theories depends on the meaning given to the expression "the knowledge of the race." Their language clearly implies that every generation has had to begin with ignorance and has had to gather by personal observation and experience all the knowledge it has ever possessed. According to this theory, there can be no progress, because each generation begins and ends just where its predecessors began and ended. Every individual has, in like manner, to pursue the same course. The knowledge acquired by others avails him nothing; he is compelled to acquire what he has by his own personal exertions.

In the nature of things, this is impossible. No generation can begin in the same place and under the same circumstances as the preceding one, for it falls heir to a large amount of capitalized facts and experiences. Its environment is necessarily different from that enjoyed by its predecessor. The atmosphere in which its first breath is drawn is charged with elements introduced into it by those who had lived and breathed before. The same is true, also, of individuals. The circumstances of their birth, the agencies active in moulding their character, and the language used by them are all made for them.

The teachings of history are also opposed to this theory of knowledge. It assures us that every generation has made considerable progress in education. But "progress can be made only on two conditions," says Cousin; "first to represent all of one's predecessors, then to be one's self; to sum up all anterior labors and to add to them."

There is a practical difficulty in the way of adopting this theory which is insuperable. Men are not able to discover all the knowledge which they need, to meet the demands of life. "Much of what is indispensably necessary for their guidance," says Dr. Payne, "they cannot learn at all, so difficult of attainment is it, and so engrossing are the special activities involved in the support of daily life. If the food eaten or the water drunk has to be analyzed, we are bound to buy, borrow or beg the knowledge or the skill of the expert."

The true theory respecting the nature of knowledge is that it includes not only all that we feel and observe but, also, all that we can reproduce of what has been felt and observed by others. The mind acquires knowledge, not by having it poured into it as water is poured into a vessel, but by its own activity. It acquires sense-knowledge by sense-activity, thought-knowledge by thought-activity, and experience-knowledge by consciousness. The Latin word "educo" comes nearer than any other term to setting forth the true process of acquiring knowledge. It means to draw out the dormant powers of the soul into active exercise.

Knowledge is the result of a mental act, or a series of mental acts.

What, it may be asked next, is the *aim of education?* This question has been variously answered by different individuals and nations, according to their surroundings and their views of life. Plato, who was a great philosopher, saw the end of education through the medium of psychology, hence declared it to be "the making of the mind the perfect instrument of thought." John Milton, who was an important factor in the political and military movements of his day, said "that the *aim* of a complete and generous education is to get men to perform justly, skillfully and magnanimously all the offices, both public and private, of peace and war." Looking at it in the light of his own philosophy, Herbert Spencer alleges that "to prepare men for complete living is the function which education has to discharge." The Jews, who had cultivated the mechanic arts more than any other nation of their day, regarded education as a means to develop more fully the handicrafts and the trades. The Phœnicians, who derived most of their living from the sea, looked upon education as the promoter of navigation and commerce. The Spartans, who were the most warlike people of Greece, declared the end of education to be the production of the best military results. The Athenians declared it to be culture, and the Romans, the highest skill in practical life. In our country, the aim of common school education is alleged to be to prepare men to become intelligent citizens.

There is some truth in all these definitions. Partaking, perhaps, too much of their surroundings, they are a little too narrow. But, divested of their personal and national considerations, the aim of education is to build up a noble character, and to qualify its possessor to discharge all the duties of the sphere in which he moves. Hence, the instruction of the undergraduate departments of our colleges and universities should seek to build up character, and that of our professional schools, to prepare men for their respective life-work.

I call attention, further, to the *qualifications* of those who are called to train the young. About all that is known of education in early times is that it was imparted by parents and priests set apart for that purpose. The qualifications of teachers have greatly varied in different ages. In the memory of many now living, the improvement in this direction has been truly amazing. "Until very recently," says a writer in the *Princeton Review*, "the public seems to have depended for schoolmasters upon the probability that there would always be some persons fit for nothing else; some lame men that could not work; some lazy men that would not work; some disabled clergyman, a physician not competent to make a living by his profession, or a lawyer waiting for a practice; some youth willing to work hard for a little money to help him on his way to his chosen calling; or some poor man unable from the lack of means to reach that end until too late in life to profit from it, and thereby compelled to make life's labor of what had been designed merely as a step thereto. To choose school-teaching from pure preference thereof and after due preparation therefor, was exceedingly rare and pertained only to the benevolent and unselfish, of whom the world has always possessed few, and never more than a few. Then the position in which the work was put by the public was calculated to make its share of that few as slender as possible. Unprovided with proper support and exposed to public obloquy, they were crushed often into penury even by the state governments, which kept down the rate of salaries to the point of starvation."

A few men far in advance of their times discovered these defects in the preparation of teachers and put forth strenuous efforts to correct them. La Salle, superintendent of public schools in France, finding it almost impossible to secure competent teachers for his schools, opened a seminary at Rheims for the express purpose of qualifying teachers for their work. A genuine normal school was established in 1792 by Lakanal, at Paris. A little later the Germans moved in the same direction. This called the attention of the nations to the much-needed reform in the education and character of schoolmasters.

Massachusetts was the first state in this country to inquire into the subject, and to inaugurate a reform. This led to the establishment of the first normal school in the United States. "Horace Mann," says Mr. Mayo, "struck the keynote of progress when he placed Father Pierce, Samuel J. May, and Tillinghast at the head of his new normal school. From that day to the present the state normal schools of New England have been under the control of a teaching faculty whose labors form one of the most instructive chapters in the history of American education." New York, New Jersey, Pennsylvania and adjacent states followed her example, until the normal school has come to be regarded as one of the most important departments of our educational system.

The establishment of these schools and the discussions connected therewith have tended very largely to improve the tone of public sentiment, and to elevate the standard of general training for teachers, but it is by no means certain that the Normal School, as we now have it, is to prove the panacea for the defects in the training of teachers. It is well known that it does not furnish the pupils with the higher studies or much culture. Its aim is to show them how to teach, and not to supply them with what to teach. If we should, on the other hand, attempt to enlarge the curriculum, and give a higher degree of culture, we should infringe on the province of state colleges and universities. It is to-day in that awkward dilemma from which it hopes sometime to be rescued. It is plain that teaching even in our lower departments requires more education and culture than our high schools afford. "Teaching," says Dr. Payne, "belongs to the higher category of intellectual employments involving broad scholarship, nice discrimination and the highest gifts of mind and heart. The knowledge which a teacher is expected to have of the workings of the pupil's mind and the best method to be used for its development is abstruse and difficult of attainment, demanding qualities of mind and educational acquirement that are far higher than the ordinary and call for thorough training as well as considerable pedagogical instruction."

This suggests the still *further question, what these pedagogical principles are.* Old-fashioned schoolmasters reduced them to two, namely, *repetition* and *memory*. They thought their pupils were making commendable progress when they could repeat their lessons by rote. School books were prepared with a view to this method, "and even the rules of grammar," in the words of another, "were put into verse to facilitate the process." Whilst this was the plan in vogue reason was largely, if not altogether, ignored, and the only stay and encouragement of the flagging memory was the birch. This plan was carried to such extremes as reached in time real absurdity. But a remedy for it was not so easily found. The first one suggested was fully as bad as the error it was intended to correct. Efforts were put forth to relieve the memory of a great part of its work, not by calling in the aid of any other faculty, but by external help, such as keys to arithmetic, and Latin school-books with interlinear translations. It was not long before it was discovered that this was a worse method than that which it proposed to mend. For a time the pupils seemed to make commendable progress, but they finally broke down altogether. The memory was taken by the shoulders and lifted bodily over its *first* difficulties, because too feeble to encounter any; by such delicate treatment and the habit of walking with crutches, its limbs were paralyzed, and it became a cripple for life. In consequence of this, the memory lost its former reputation. Stories of its feats in other days began to seem apocryphal; and the next step was to discard it altogether.

The reaction which took place in the theory of *repetition* and *memory* was followed by the age of reason, when everything was addressed to the understanding. The school-room was invaded by philosophers; and instead of the knowledge of things the reasons for them were exacted of the opening mind. Arguments were to be framed before the pupil had possession of the material to argue with. The absurdity of this plan may not have appeared to its framers, but it did to those who undertook to execute it.

Happily the reign of infant philosophers is largely, if not wholly, *over*. A better day has dawned. The conclusion has, at last, been reached that children are not memories with material attachments to be impressed with the rod; that they are not born logicians with capacities for reasoning without data; but human beings with souls of the same kind as those of adults, only undeveloped, comprehending the faculties of memory, reason, sensation and emotion which, in order to be rightly educated, must be educated together; that they are also moral as well as intellectual beings; and that they have bodies upon the health of which depends, to a great degree, the progress of the whole.

The conception of education which is becoming general in our day, assumes that the *what* and the *how* of teaching must be adapted to the capability of the pupils, that they must be changed as those capabilities grow ; that they must follow the order of the activity of the mental powers ; that they must aim at a harmonious development of the whole man ; and that all this is to be done by occasioning the quickening of the activity of the pupil's mind. Consequently, a course of early training should include all the departments of elementary knowledge in order to give the mind a harmonious development, thus preparing it to acquire all kinds of knowledge and to resist the narrowing tendencies of the occupation in which he shall be engaged in after life.

The only other point connected with education which I shall mention is its *relation to religion*. Can the youth of the land be prepared to perform their full duty as citizens and members of society without the aid of religious principles and precepts? This is the grave question of the day. It is that which is threatening the permanency of the public school system and the peace of our country. It is a matter of history that it has been thought through the ages that education and religion are one and indivisible. This opinion is not the offspring of superstition and ignorance, but a logical deduction from the nature of the *object* to be educated, the means of education, and the facts of experience. The object to be developed and trained is the *mind*. This is not a well-watered garden, divided into grass-plots, parterres, and flower-beds that are sufficiently independent of each other to admit of different cultivators of the soil, diversities of seed, and various modes of irrigation. Nor is it, like the human body, endowed with organs so remotely connected with each other as to allow of the training of one or two without materially affecting others. The soul is a *unit*. Its faculties are not distinct and independent entities, but modes of operation. They are placed so closely together that no one can materially and permanently affect one without influencing the others. It is impossible to enlighten the understanding without increasing the sensitiveness of the conscience; to influence the will without training the emotions and the affections; to increase the power of the memory without quickening the consciousness which takes cognizance of the facts of experience; and to develop properly the intellectual powers without cultivating the moral. To attempt this would be to neglect the man himself and train some of his powers; to arrest every process of thought before reaching its legitimate conclusion and do violence to the reasoning powers. Every line of true knowledge finds its completeness in the great First Cause, even as every beam of daylight leads the eye to the sun.

The means of education are so interwoven that no power on earth can separate them. Schools can not be carried on without discipline, but discipline must be based on right and wrong. What is the standard? Rewards and punishments are resorted to everywhere as incentives to study, but these derive their value from merit and demerit; what lies at their foundation? History must be taught, or we shall separate ourselves from the past with its manifold valuable lessons, but how can the history of Continental Europe be taught without explaining the revival of letters and the Reformation of the sixteenth century? Who could teach the growth and great power of England without saying something about the religion of the people? It would be impossible to tell the descendants of the Huguenots, whence their ancestors came, and how it happened that they left sunny France for the wilds of North Carolina, without referring to the Edict of Nantes and the massacre of St. Bartholomew. No fair-minded scientist could undertake to expound the theories entertained concerning the origin of the globe without calling his pupil's attention to that contained in the Mosaic cosmogony. Would any man worthy to be intrusted with the education of immortal beings attempt to explain the origin of the race without intimating that it had been held for six thousand years that God created man in his own image? These things cannot be separated. The truths of the Christian religion are so pervading, so closely connected with morality, so interwoven with social and civil polity, and so diffused through all literature that it can not be banished from our schools.

Then the facts of experience abundantly show that the separation of religion from education involves *positive evil* to society. The effort in France, Holland, Great Britain and America to exclude the Bible from the common schools is a step towards bringing up in infidelity and atheism all that part of the population dependent on those schools for their education. For, "a choice here," as another has said, "is not between religion and no religion, but between religion and irreligion, between Christianity and infidelity. The mere negative of *theism* is *atheism*. There is no middle ground between them. This is the view taken of it by Daniel Webster in his great speech on Girard College. "It is all idle," he remarks, "it is a mockery and an insult to common sense, to maintain that a school for the instruction of youth from which Christian instruction by Christian teachers is sedulously and vigorously shut out, is not deistical and infidel in its purpose and tendency." Dr. Miner, another authority on educational matters, says, "it is one of the most remarkable phenomena of our perverted humanity that among a Christian people and in a Protestant land, such a decision as whether the education of youth may not be secularized, should not seem as absurd as to inquire whether school-rooms should be located under water or in darksome caverns."

At no time and by no nation, until recently, was separation of education and religion thought to be possible. "In what age, by what sect, where, when, by whom," asks Mr. Webster, "has religious truth been excluded from the education of youth? Nowhere, never," is his emphatic reply. "Everywhere and at all times it has been regarded essential, for religion is of the essence and vitality of useful instruction."

Whilst the great majority of the people of France, Holland, Great Britain and the United States admit all that has been said, yet the fact remains that the public school education in all these countries is rapidly becoming secularized. The instruction of the young is passing from the church to the state. It promises to be ere long one of the functions of the latter. In a country like ours, where a large number of conflicting creeds are cherished, it is the duty of the civil authorities to devise an educational system that will not interfere with the rights nor clash with the religious views of those interested in the subject. Simple justice shows that the state cannot tax parents for the support of schools that teach doctrines which they do not believe, or compel children to attend upon a course of instruction which they abhor. A large number of the tax-payers and supporters of our public schools believe, on the other hand, that education unsupported by the principles of religion, must be of little value. What, then, is to be done? Will the parents who are the natural guardians of the children and who are consequently primarily responsible for their education and training undertake the task in primitive style and teach them everything they choose? This is not practicable and the state can not afford to leave the education of its citizens in uncertainty. Will the church, the next party responsible for the education of the young, undertake the work? She has not the means necessary to do it well. She can not compel attendance, or claim, as her own, multitudes of children that are to be educated. In self-defence, therefore, the state must see that all her citizens receive a sufficient amount of education to perform their civil duties.

Here arises the most difficult educational question of our day. How can we preserve our public school system, and yet meet the demands of multitudes of Christian parents and the claims of the different branches of the Christian church? The division of the school funds is not to be thought of. The complete secularization of public instruction, on the other hand, would be an outrage to which the majority of our people will never submit. What then? The issue is squarely before us. Shall not concessions be made that will prove satisfactory to both sides? Does the religious party ask too much of the state when it demands the introduction of ethics into its curriculum? This is not religion but philosophy; the source of its principles is not the Christian Scriptures, but the human constitution and that of society at large. Since the Bible, as the Supreme Court of Wisconsin has recently and justly declared, is not sectarian, or the religious creed of any denomination, but a thesaurus of the highest ethical principles known to the world, why may it not be read in all our schools? Is the state, on the other hand, asking too much of parents, when it tells them to see to the religious part of their children's education at home? or of the church, when it offers her an opportunity to send men at stated times, as in England, to furnish her youth with the religious instruction she wishes them to have? May not an adjustment of this sort serve to keep our public school system from injury, and meet, at the same time, the views, and satisfy the conscientious scruples, of those who do not believe in the possibility of divorcing religion and education without disastrous results? The solution of this question demands all the sagacity of our best statesmen, all the discretion of the leaders of public opinion, all the skill of our educators, and all the Christian forbearance of every branch of the Church of Christ in our land.

PURPOSES OF THE STUDY OF LATIN.

BY NATHANIEL BUTLER, JR., A. M., PROFESSOR OF LATIN, UNIVERSITY OF ILLINOIS, CHAMPAIGN.

Has the study of Latin any legitimate place in a course of training and instruction adapted to the needs of the present time? That question can hardly be decided on the authority of those who have entered into its discussion, because on both sides are found men with equal claim to respectful hearing. That the study has *a value* no one denies; but those who advise that it be dropped claim that other studies are valuable in the same directions and for the same purposes, and that these others have, in addition, practical and scientific values, by virtue of which they should altogether displace the study of Latin.

If Latin is to hold its place, this claim must be met, and it must be shown that the study is valuable, not only in a general way, as many other studies are valuable, as a tonic and invigorator of the mind, but that this study has a function in education peculiar to itself, and that its removal from the courses of the schools would leave those courses incomplete.

I believe that this is true. Freely admitting that we do not live in a literary age; that the spirit of the time is scientific, practical, realistic; and that the demands made upon educated men are very different from those made even twenty-five years ago, still it is my belief that the study of Latin is an important factor in the preparation of men and women for *these very demands*.

We maintain this view without in any sense arraying ourselves against the spirit of the time. We must all rejoice in the "new education." We should have no wish to recall days the when it was believed that classical education was the only education. The splendid revelations of the sciences, the countless benefits they have conferred upon human life, the extent to which they have made us masters of the world about us, and familiar with the worlds above us, the influence of scientific study in unfolding and stimulating the mind of the student and the investigator—all these attest, that outside the realm of classical literature a field is open for the human mind in which its activity may have full play, its powers be taxed to the utmost, and in which it may secure results of the highest practical value. We should not wish to restrain men and women from entering this field. Its labors are noble, the results are tangible and important, the rewards are immediate. It is natural and right that men and women should incline toward it. It is also right and natural that courses of study intended to prepare men and women for such activity should aim to embrace whatever is especially helpful, and to exclude whatever has no direct part to play in fitting the student for what is before him. Every study that holds a place in the curriculum should be made to stand, and show cause why it should not be removed.

It is well for us to remember, however, in passing upon the various studies, that while the times make many new demands upon young men and women, it is, after all, *men* and *women* that are needed, and not merely human machines; that the grand results to which science points with just pride, wrought as they were by mechanical skill and technical knowledge, were not wrought by mechanical skill and technical knowledge alone, but by these directed by clearness of thought and accuracy of judgment. It has been well said that even an engine is *brains* and iron. Some things which are neither directly mechanical nor directly technical may be important elements of a mechanical or technical education. For success in a specialty there are certain things which a man must master, not directly connected with that specialty—things which underlie every specialty, just as sound physical health underlies all physical activity.

It is the purpose of this paper to show what, in the opinion of the writer, are the results to be gained in the study of Latin, and thus, if possible, to answer the question, "Shall we retain Latin in our modern courses of study?" It is not intended to enter upon an exhaustive discussion of this study, but only to call attention to some of its more practical and immediate uses—uses which nothing else so well fulfills. I wish to dwell upon three points: *First*, the relation of the study of Latin to command of English. *Second*, the relation of the study of Latin to the scientific habit of mind. *Third*, the value of the matter, the substance, the thought, contained in the Latin classics.

1. Regarding the mastery of English, then, we shall all agree that whatever a man's work may be, he can hardly stand in greater need of anything than the ability to use his own language with ease and exactness—to say readily, naturally, and clearly what he means. Not merely for the needs of the editor, the author, the professional man, but for the every-day uses of life, the purposes of correspondence, or of ordinary verbal interchange of thought, mastery of one's own language is a most practical and necessary accomplishment. I do not refer, at this point, to familiarity with the subject of English literature, as such, nor of English philology, but to the mastery of English as an instrument of every-day practical use—the mastery of the art of transferring thought from mind to mind by means of clear and simple speech.

This art is almost as rare as it is necessary. One has only to have a large general correspondence, or to read our daily prints, or to listen to the average public speaker, to realize the painful lack of the simple qualities of clearness and completeness in the thought and speech of men. It is as rare as it is refreshing to find a man or woman whose sentences are natural and at the same time perfectly clear and complete. The mistakes, misunderstandings, blunders, in affairs ranging in importance from the arrangement of the household to the running of railway trains, are largely due to the lack of clear and precise interchange of thought between man and man. Whether a man directs a gang of laborers or stands in a pulpit, or controls the movements of an army, or manages a commercial business, no accomplishment is more needful than that of habitual clearness of thought and expression. It is a just remark of a recent writer in the Atlantic Monthly that "there is no pursuit in which an American does not often need to use English easily and well."

It is the gaining of this practical accomplishment, the fuller mastery of the art of language, which, in my judgment, is one of the chief purposes to be secured in the study of Latin. And it is at precisely this point that the study of classics (both Latin and Greek) has been most sharply assailed. Mr. Charles Francis Adams, in his famous Phi Beta Kappa address, complains that he and his contemporaries at Harvard, though students of Latin and Greek, were not trained to follow out a line of sustained, close thought, and to express themselves in clear, concise terms. They were trained neither to speak nor to express thought. A similar complaint is made by a writer in the *North American Review*, who charges that among the products of the American classical system it is difficult to find one writer "who has learned to drape the graceful garment of language around the firm body of an idea." (Clarence King, *North American Review*, October, 1888). Both these writers, however, make the methods, not the study, the object of attack. And it must be confessed that the complaint is largely just. Certainly in my time at college, the study of Latin consisted mainly in committing to memory lists of rules and exceptions in the grammar, and then puzzling out at hap-hazard a certain amount of Latin text each day, not for the purpose of reading the author with some intelligent grasp of his thought, nor for drill in making good English sentences, but chiefly for applying the rules of grammar. I remember distinctly that, in reading Cæsar or Cicero, I carried along from day to day no idea of connected narrative or argument. I might just as well have been digging out a section of Cæsar on one day, of Nepos the next, of Sallust the third, and the next day of Livy. The problem was simply and only this, to puzzle some Latin sentences into English, and then, as the supreme end of study, tack to each word and clause the suitable grammatical label. The grammar was not looked upon as an aid to reading the author, but the author was regarded as a convenient means of applying grammatical rules. We utterly failed to catch the spirit of the author; our translations had no life and little sense. We were not studying the art of language; much less were we studying literature; we studied grammatical analysis. The method was wrong, and it was paralyzing to thought and expression. Mr. Clarence King has well said that "a free and joyous flow of language, the subtle ceremony of marrying words to ideas so that they forever go hand in hand as one, can no more be learned by grammatical analysis, than the secret of life can be learned among the severed fragments in a dissecting room." But this very writer touches the root of the matter when, avowing his respectful devotion to classic letters and arts, he says, "it is only the American *method* that he laments and pities." If the ends proposed have been mainly committing to memory lists of rules and exceptions in the grammars, and guessing at the meaning of the text for the one purpose of applying the rules *after the sense has been guessed out*,—if these have been the ends in view, who can wonder that the results were real harm to the student, and that the methods have fallen under the condemnation of thoughtful men?

But taught as it should be, learned as it ought to be, I believe that there is no instruction better than Latin for the mastery of the art of language in general and of the English language in particular.

Consider for a moment the material about which the mind occupies itself in the study of Latin. Here we have the language and literature of a people whose characteristics were law, order, discipline—a people who were eminently direct and practical. These traits, of course, impressed themselves upon the language they spoke. Accordingly, we find the Latin style marked by order, exactness, completeness. Every word, every phrase, every clause has a definite function, a clear relation. Even though the sentence be long and involved, it is complete and its structure perfect. The problem of the student is to catch the precise meaning of the sentence and to express that meaning in equivalent English; to make the English sentence say just what the Latin says, and to say it as well as the Latin said it. The performance of this task requires clearness, accuracy, and completeness both in understanding and in expression. The student who, day by day, is turning the pages of Cicero or Horace into the very best English at his command, who has learned to handle with ease one of Cæsar's page-long sentences, or to complete Juvenal's ellipses, who has learned to translate Latin authors idiomatically, fluently, has enjoyed a very special kind of training in the arts of clear thinking and speaking. Good English is not a science to be learned from books on rhetoric; it is an art to be mastered by use. The student of Latin is daily making English sentences with admonitions in every Latin sentence against the very faults he is most in need of correcting, He is daily learning, in the most practical way, to do just what Mr. Adams complains he was not trained to do: to "follow out a line of sustained, close thought, expressing himself in clear, concise terms."

This point is well made by Cruttwell, in his "History of Roman Literature." "The utility of Roman literature," says he, "may be sought in the practical standard of its thought, and in the almost faultless correctness of its composition. * * * The latter excellence fits it above all for an educational use. There is probably no language which in that respect comes near to it. * * Among Roman classical authors, scarce a sentence can be detected which offends against logical accuracy, or defies critical analysis. In this respect Latin authors stand alone." Even Greek is different. "The powerful intellect of an Æschylus or a Thucydides did not prevent them from transgressing laws which in their day were undiscovered, and which their own writings helped to form. Nor in modern times could we find a single language in which the idioms of the best writers could be reduced to conformity with strict rule. French, which at first sight seems to offer such an instance, is seen, on a closer view, to be fuller of illogical idioms than any other language. * * * English, at least in its older forms, abounds in special idioms, and German is still less likely to be adduced. As long, therefore, as penetrating insight into syntax [sentence structure] is considered desirable, so long will Latin offer the best field for obtaining it."

That this result may be accomplished, let the student of Latin understand that he is studying the practical art of language, and not the science of grammar. Let his attention be fixed upon the task of catching the author's meaning, and so rendering it that it shall make the same impression on the English mind that it did on that of a Roman. Let him understand that it is for this very purpose that he needs a most thorough knowledge of the grammar. Thus it will be to him a *working* knowledge and not a merely theoretical. The forms of words must be recognized at sight, the syntax of the language must be completely understood, and the unceasing grammatical drill required will do the student no harm, if he is made to see in it, not an end in itself, but a means of reading the literature.

The most serious complaint against classical study has arisen from a strange and unnatural reversing of this principle. When a stone building is to be erected, the stones are prepared at a quarry, often thousands of miles away. But they are sent to the place where the building is to stand, each bearing a mark for the guidance of the builder, telling him just what part each has in the structure. The syntax of each stone is plainly marked upon it. Now suppose that the builder utterly disregards these marks, and falls to work to find out the place of each stone by trying it here and trying it there, and guessing and inferring as best he can. That would represent the way in which much of our translation used to be done. But, worse than that. After the builder has guessed his building together let him *then* be required to take it down, piece by piece, and explain the marks on the stones—marks which he has never thought of noticing while he was putting up the house. He explains the characters, leaves the stones scattered about, and goes on to undertake a new contract. So with the Latin student, studying after the old system. He guesses his sentence together, and *then* breaks it up in order to explain the marks that are on every word for his guidance. This is to reverse the process and defeat the ends of language study. We should train our pupils to use their knowledge of etymology and syntax, not for analysis, but for synthesis, not for taking the sentence apart, but for putting the sentence together. The student's knowledge of grammar, *after the first year*, should avail him the instant he encounters a sentence, and not only after he has puzzled out the meaning. The grammar should be his guide to an intelligent reading of the author, and not a tax upon memory or ingenuity. The sight of an *ut* or a *cum*, a *si* or a *quod* at the beginning of a clause, the sight of a subjunctive or an infinitive, an accusative or an ablative, should be his clue to the sense. Trained in this way the pupil will see that a Latin sentence is not to be guessed out by a more or less ingenious combination of the words, but that he is to read it as a Roman boy read it, from the first word to the last *in the Roman order*. There should be no picking out the words, no changing of the original order. The forms of the words are to show the reader their relations and meaning. In this way he feels that he is in contact with the mind of his author, he catches his spirit, and the drudgery of translation is changed to a positive pleasure.

Of course this translating in the Latin order is only for the first reading, in which the purpose is to catch the precise thought and sentiment of the author; it will then be in order to turn into equivalent idiomatic English.

If Latin be read in this way the study will no longer be chargeable with concerning itself only to train the memory by learning rules and exceptions in the grammars. For such reading of Latin taxes continually the student's power of accurate observation; it calls for a strong and commanding use of intelligent judgment; it trains him to the habit of clear and sustained thought, and of simple and complete expression. He is really using his mind in a way to make him respect himself and the literature he studies. Read in this way, I believe that Latin can do for a boy's English what nothing else can do. Better than anything else it will teach him the art of sentence-making.

I have tried to point out that Latin is especially fitted for an instrument of training in the use of English, because of its wonderfully perfect sentence structure, its style being such as is most sure to impress on the style of the student the characters of clearness, accuracy, and completeness. But besides this perfect sentence structure, Latin has another and perhaps even more direct relation to the student's practical understanding, and working knowledge of English. There is an important sense in which Latin itself is not a dead language. It has modern and present uses. It is the mother tongue of the languages of Southwestern Europe. It furnishes forty-five per cent. of the words in our own language. A very large proportion of the words used in scientific nomenclature are directly from the Latin. A knowledge of Latin has, therefore, a direct bearing upon the mastery of some of the most important of the languages now spoken by civilized peoples. Of course, if one desires a speaking knowledge of a language he should live where that language is spoken. But there can scarcely be better preparation for a thoroughly intelligent *reading* acquaintance with the languages of modern Southern Europe than thorough study of Latin. I speak of this because a reading knowledge of these languages is now regarded as a necessary part of a practical education.

But I am chiefly concerned with Latin as related to English. In addition, then, to its use in promoting clearness of thought and expression in sentence construction, I mention again the fact that of the words in the English dictionary, forty-five per cent. are of Latin origin. This proportion does not include such terms —which are nevertheless thoroughly adopted into our family—as *caveat, ex post facto, retroactive, sine die, habeas corpus, ipse dixit, ipso facto, in toto, sub rosa;* besides these, many words have come into English without change. "Candidate," "suffrage," "legal," "legitimate," "veto," "civil," "suburban," "confiscate," are examples of a large class of words that are equally Latin and English. It is self-evident that a man who has become sensitive to the force and meaning of such words in the original will use them with greater intelligence and effectiveness in his own language.

But, more than this : Latin words are built up from roots and stems by a regular process which the student can easily learn, so that the very form of the word has a meaning in the English derivative that it has in the Latin original. Thus he learns that the ending -*arium* denotes a place where something is found or kept. Knowing that *liber* means a book he has no need to look in the lexicon to know that *librarium* means a place where books are kept. In the same way he knows at a glance that *apiarium* is a place for bees ; *aviarium*, a place for birds ; *aquarium*, a water-tank. Thus he finds himself recognizing the fundamental meaning of familiar words. *Librarium* becomes "library"; *aviarium*, "aviary"; *aquarium* is transferred to English unchanged. The syllable *-or*, applied to a certain part of the verb, denotes the doer of the act. Knowing this he feels at once the force of this ending applied: *ago*, "I do"; *oro*, "I speak"; *imitor*, "I imitate"; giving the Latin words—which are English as well—"actor," "orator," "imitator." When he has learned that the ending *-tas* or *-itas* denotes an abstract noun, he needs no lexicon to inform him that *honestas* means "honesty"; *veritas*, "verity"; *æquitas*, "equity"; and the peculiar force of these English abstracts is familiar to him, as he involuntarily associates them with the adjectives from which they are derived. The list might be indefinitely prolonged of English words whose very *form* displays their force and meaning in a way that cannot be understood or felt by one not familiar with Latin. Word-study, and especially tracing the line from Latin words to their English progeny, should form a prominent feature of the study of Latin. It opens up the real treasures of English as nothing else can do. It never fails to interest; and, while it enriches the student's knowledge of English, it also bears directly upon ease in reading the literature; for, in giving him a working vocabulary, it does away with the necessity of constantly turning the leaves of the lexicon—a tax upon the attention and a waste of time.

2. In addition to what has been said of the value of Latin, resulting from its perfect sentence structure, and from the extent to which it enters into modern European languages, into the language of science, and into the English vocabulary, I wish to say a word about the value of the study in establishing the scientific habit of mind, of which we hear so much nowadays—that is to say, the habit of exact observation and correct inference—a habit needful in every science, and, indeed, in every relation of life. For this purpose the study is useful from the day when it is begun by the lad of twelve or thirteen. At the very outset he learns that

regina means one thing, that *reginam* means another, that *reginarum* means still another. He learns that *laudo* has a different meaning from *laudavit*, and so on. He sees that the root of the word does not change, but that syllables joined to the root do change, and that he must judge the meaning of the word by noting these added syllables. He begins at the very outset to observe and to infer. But further, the Latin has, as we have already said, a remarkable system of word building. Certain word roots are capable of many modifications of meaning through the attachment of significant endings. The mastery of these significant endings is not difficult; and while their ultimate use is to assist the reader, by displaying the meaning of the word the instant the eye falls upon it, yet that very perception of the meaning trains in the habit of accurate observation and correct inference. Latin word-building is just as much a science as is zoölogy or chemistry. Properly conducted, it establishes the same habit of mind. The same is true of word-inflections. The boy who is learning to recognize the marks of case, number, mood, and tense, or to perceive the force of significant derivative endings, is going through precisely the same mental process as when he classifies minerals or shells, or names his botanical specimens at sight. This sort of training is most important during the first two years of the study of Latin, at a time before the student has begun science; and in this way boys of thirteen to sixteen may be led to form habits that will be most useful to them when they reach the work of the laboratory. I have made actual and repeated test of the validity of this claim for Latin by appeals to the experience of professors and students in our scientific courses, and I am satisfied that it constitutes one of the strongest arguments in favor of that study. This, too, I set over against Mr. Adams' objection that the classics failed to train the powers of observation—an objection that was doubtless just, as urged against the system prevalent in his college days. Of the importance of this early systematic training President Hyde, of Bowdoin College, says in the December (1888) *Atlantic Monthly*: "The chief value of a classical [preparatory] course lies not in what its students know when they graduate, but in what it enables them to learn afterward. * * * Its aim is to form right mental habits. It insists on accuracy, thoroughness and form."

This scientific word-study, like the study of syntax and the tracing of English derivatives, gives the student a familiar working knowledge of the language, and so leads directly to ease and sympathy in translation. This result should appear early. If the right method is employed from the first, the student ought, after the beginning of the Freshman year, to be able to read with relish the authors of the classical period, as they come in course; and his evident pleasure, the activity of his mind, and his steadily-increasing command of English, gained in daily translation, would set at rest all doubts about the utility of the study.

3. I do not mean to speak at length of the value of Latin literature as literature—of the value of what is here offered to the thought and feeling of the student. Its value is recognized, and if it has not been felt—if the thought and feeling of the student have not been kindled—we must again say that the fault has lain in the method which has pointed the student to the grammar and not to the literature. Not by chance have these writings survived. They are literature in the highest sense. As Simcox has pointed out, "the Latin authors wrote under a strong regard for all that tends to promote fellow feeling among mankind. Latin literature throughout assumes and enforces social rights and duties." The Romans were, among the nations of history, pre-eminently practical. They were the traders, politicians, law-makers of the time, and as such easily the peers of moderns. The lives and writings of Cicero, Cato, Gracchus, Crassus, are full of lessons for our own times. The tone of Roman literature is essentially modern, and highly stimulating to the modern mind. Horace is

greater than Pope; Juvenal is more stimulating than Swift; Tacitus is as refined as Irving; and it may be doubted whether Grant or Sherman will ever be read and admired by so many as Cæsar. It is hardly necessary to call attention to the development which the student's judgment must receive in passing upon the character of Roman society, culture, and politics, from which modern times have received so large an inheritance. It is taken for granted that this will follow an intelligent reading of the text; that when the student has fully grasped the author's meaning he will be encouraged to criticise, to commend or condemn, and that he will be directed to collateral reading.

No, not only because of its value as language study, not only for its value as an instrument for training, but because of what it can do for thought and feeling, we cannot afford to spare Roman literature from the curriculum. There is in it a freshness, a sincerity, a genuineness, which it is most helpful to touch. It is this that we love, it is this that helps us in Chaucer and in Shakespeare, and in every singer or prophet. Horace, Virgil, Juvenal, Persius, Tacitus, all have it. Let the student feel it, become acquainted with it, catch it. It has for us what we need in these days *along with* our intense absorption in the real. This age of railways and bridges, of machinery and tools, is a glorious age. This magnificent building, flooded at night with the splendor of the day, these wonderful means of travel and communication all about us, tell their own story. Yet these grand results exist for what is grander than them all—*men* and *women*. Let us never reverse this truth, and suppose that we were made for these things. They were made for us; and nothing should we less desire than that our children become alive to the things about them and dead to the world within them. Let us exalt and teach the knowledge of this material world, but never let us forget the yet higher world of mind and character. Some one has well said, "I would rather my son thought that the sun goes round the earth, than that he

be devoid of high thought, noble impulse, true feeling."
We are sometimes told that action, not thought and feeling are the true end of man. True. But also *fruits*, not roots, are the true end of an orchard. Yet we can have no fruits without roots. No, we commit a fallacy when we array the worker against the thinker, when we talk about acts rather than thoughts. The union of the two can alone be fruitful. The two elements must go hand in hand. If we would avoid a narrow and defective culture, we must learn to call practical that which trains to right habits of thought and feeling, as well as that which trains to the right use of hand and eye.

This seems to be the view of the most thoughtful advocates of the "New Education," as distinguished from the "Old Education." Mr. Charles Francis Adams, already quoted, says explicitly: "I am no believer in that narrow scientific and technological training which now and again we hear extolled. A practical and too often a mere vulgar money-making utility seems to be its natural outcome." In the same line, a recent writer in the New York *Independent*, referring to the new methods of classical teaching — methods pointing the student to natural and familiar acquaintance with his author, instead of filling him with fear of the grammar — goes on to say: "And this will mean the permanence of the classics in their commanding position in the schools. Labored methods and halting, meager results, have been the main arguments against these studies." But these methods may be corrected so that "to the discipline that seems to belong preëminently to classical study, may be added this advantage of a permanent familiarity with noble and ennobling literature." And, finally, Mr. King, in the *North American Review*, writing in derision of the old-time classical course, declares the classics, both Greek and Latin, capable of performing the highest educational function when he says: "Ours is a vulgar but remarkably active civilization, given over for the most part to the energetic pursuit of personal prosperity and the struggle for material good. Of all ages and lands this is the one where, for the mind's and soul's sake, a brilliant struggle must be made to stem the almost irresistible current of sodden materialism. After that highest of all ideals and idealizing forces, a pure and spiritual religion, there is nothing comparable to the classics for the exaltation of intellectual and artistic standards, which forever transcend that crushed, distorted, warped and blasted thing, that sweet, splendid, grotesque, droll, dreadful thing — the real."

"Taught as they might be, learned as they should be, so that not the mechanism of dialects only, but the splendid ideality of antique thought and feeling, may become a part of the young nation, the lofty classics of the Greeks and Romans can be made of inestimable value in the creation of American character."

THE COLLEGE PHASE OF THE NEW EDUCATION.

BY REV. E. A. TANNER, D. D., PRESIDENT OF ILLINOIS COLLEGE, JACKSONVILLE.

A generation, covering from thirty to thirty-three years, by common agreement is distributed into four periods of nearly equal length. The average child of seven or eight years has come to such practical knowledge of right and wrong, that we consider him accountable for his choice of good or evil, in his ordinary experiences. At from fourteen to sixteen, he reaches puberty. This transition period the civil law recognizes as "the age of consent." At twenty-one, the state acknowledges manhood and welcomes to all the responsibilities of citizenship. From that time, life, whether long or short, is an absolute individuality. I lay no great stress upon this doctrine of sevens, though I do believe there is in it something more than mere chance, or fancy. The first division comes from long experience in the moral training of the race. The second is the natural suggestion of physiology. The third is sanctioned by the teachings of psychology and social science. The fourth is the resultant of the other three. I mention this well-known distribution chiefly, however, to call attention to some peculiar drifts of modern thought.

Our new theology, if self-consistent, must *raise the age of moral responsibility*, in order to give childhood the fairest chance. Our new sociology demands that the *age of consent shall be raised*, for the protection of purity. But our new education faces the other way, and, in the name of moral and intellectual progress, demands that restrictions shall be removed, and that *the age of choice shall be lowered*, so as to cover not only the courses of the university, but likewise all the studies of the college.

Great confusion in discussion arises from the fact that no distinction is drawn between the college and the university. We have in the United States a multitude of institutions which are colleges in name and in function. We have a multitude of institutions, which are universities in name, and colleges in function. We have a few institutions which are universities in name, and partly colleges and partly universities in function. We have not a single institution which is a university in name and solely a university in function. Johns Hopkins approaches nearest to this last description. She is eager to realize this ideal as soon as possible, but she is obliged for the present to maintain a college department. Johns Hopkins was founded as a pure university. Her trustees and faculty regard the collegiate part of their work as a necessary evil, from which they are to be freed at a very early day. Harvard and Yale were founded as colleges. They have made their reputation as colleges. They are passing slowly and reluctantly from college to university work. They still make the college the center of activity. But the sooner they abandon college work and devote themselves exclusively to university work, the better it will be for the interests of the higher learning.

Yale is moving so cautiously in the direction of electives, that she has not harmed the general cause of college education throughout the country. The same cannot be said of Harvard. The revolution which she seeks to effect, is, to obliterate every distinction, and to subject the whole American college system to the methods of the German University. She insists that the absolute freedom of manhood shall be given to every boy in his teens, who is sufficiently advanced in learning to enter the freshman class. It is true that a few of the studies of the first year are still required at Harvard, but it is openly proclaimed that they will presently disappear.

It is the proper province of the college to deal with immature young men between the ages of eighteen and twenty-two. It is the proper province of the university to take those same young men, after they have reached maturity, and prepare them for their special work in life. We all agree that so soon as a man passes out of college into the university, he should be perfectly free to pursue any study which he may desire; that, in choosing his vocation, he should be at liberty to follow any line of investigation which he deems profitable. A true university should furnish facilities for the mastery of any and every branch of knowledge. A true university should be a place for unlimited original research, and a place for imparting to every one who desires it, and whenever he desires it, the accumulated learning of all the ages. Such a university should say to its students, "I open to you the opportunity to enter any and every realm of inquiry, but I have no suggestions for your guidance in selection, you must take the whole responsibility for every choice, for your methods of study, and for your manner of life. You are accountable to me for nothing. I leave you to yourself, without a single restriction, to work out your own destiny." So far the old education and the new are in perfect accord. But, not content with this, the new education insists that the principle of unrestricted choice, which all admit should be the law of the university, should be carried down into the college, and should govern the whole curriculum.

Now, while the old education is ready to concede that it is wise to admit the elective system into our colleges, it stoutly maintains that it is necessary to confine its workings to the upper classes, and to guard against its abuse even there. Conservative men believe that a back-bone of required studies should extend through the curriculum, that even juniors and seniors should not be left wholly to themselves in their choices. But the fight waxes hottest over the position of the new education, that sophomores and even freshmen shall be permitted to study what they choose and as they choose, with very little direct control by college authorities. Against this doctrine many of our wisest men enter a solemn protest in the name of sound morality and of liberal learning. This method would subvert the historic conception of the purpose of college training. It has been, and it should continue to be, the chief aim of the college, not to impart a mass of information on any particular subject, but to discipline the intellectual faculties for any and every kind of activity. In the college course discipline is essential, information incidental. In the university course information is of primary and discipline of secondary importance.

To give the young man this mastery of his mental powers, which is the function of the college, three things and three only are necessary. He must be taught to *observe*, to *think* and to *express his thought*. He will then be ready to graduate and to enter the university, there to employ his faculties in the acquisition of such knowledge of a technical or professional nature as will be most serviceable in his chosen vocation.

It is obvious that there is nothing else so good as the natural sciences to train the powers of observation. Furthermore, a few of the sciences may be selected which will answer this purpose in all cases, as well as if every man should make his own choice. It is sheer nonsense to claim that, for the uses which the college should subserve, a wide range of electives in science is of any substantial benefit to the student.

In the second place, it is manifest that mathematics, leading to logic and psychology, must continue to be the chief reliance for developing the power of orderly and protracted thought. Here also there is not needed in the college curriculum a great variety of electives.

In the third place, argument is not required to prove that the study of language is the natural method to acquire the power of expression. And the college which selects and prescribes such languages as experience has proved to be the best adapted to this purpose, will do its legitimate work as a college, better than an institution which could give its students their option among all the tongues of Babel.

An institution with a faculty of ten men, with classes of moderate size and with three well-digested prescribed courses, will do as excellent college work, as Johns Hopkins is doing to-day with her seven carefully prescribed courses. Such multiplicity makes a great display, but for practical purposes it is worthless. Again, Williams College, which is comparatively poor in electives, is to-day, with her prescribed courses, giving her students more valuable college training than is Harvard, with her bewildering parade of electives and the almost unbounded liberty which she promises her youngest boys.

The provinces of knowledge have greatly multiplied, and the new education claims that the demands upon the colleges have increased in the same proportion, but that claim is untenable. The demands upon the universities have increased in the same proportion, and they will continue so to increase. The colleges, however, have been comparatively little affected. The universities must furnish new instruction in every department, but the colleges only need to select from many new branches here and there one, which is better for discipline, or which is equally good for discipline and at the same time more valuable for information.

Let me emphasize the idea that the liberty to choose between three wisely prescribed courses is, for all the legitimate purposes of college training, as valuable as the liberty to choose among thirty such courses; and that the offer of a dozen wisely selected electives is better than the offer of a hundred miscellaneous electives. The simple fact is, that the wants of all minds between the ages of 18 and 22 are so nearly the same, that there is no need of that great diversity of full courses, or of separate studies, on which such stress is laid by the apostles of the new education. Let us not be carried away by the great parade of optionals, offered to our boys.

In the next place, the average freshman is not competent to make the best selection. He does not know what will give him greatest mental power, and, if he did know, he would usually choose, instead, that which is easiest, or that for which he has a passing fancy. Your boy at college is just like your boy at home. He needs general direction, day by day. To make him his own master at 17 or 18 would often be quick ruin. Though you gradually give him freer rein, would you dare to surrender all directing power, much before he reached his majority? I appeal to the teachings of general experience in family training. The great secret of bringing your boy safely, wisely and successfully to his majority, is to establish in childhood a considerate but firm control of your will over his will, and then to relax that control little by little, in proportion as you discern on his part a growing ability to decide what is best, and a growing disposition to choose in accordance with the dictates of reason. I appeal to you who are householders, and who have living at home, sons under the age of twenty, to know whether it is best for society, whether it is best for your family, whether it is best for yourselves, whether it is best for the young men *themselves*, that every restriction should be swept away, and that they should be left to unconditional freedom of choice and action. To this, sensible fathers and mothers can make but one answer. Now, that which is not best for those boys at home, is not best at college. The mere transfer from the one place to the other does not suddenly mature the judgment and bring deliverance from caprice and passion. A wise father will retain in his own hand a certain measure of authority until the son's majority, though the last years of that boy's minority will be chiefly self-directive. This general law of the household should be the general law of the college. Such is the harmonious teaching of common sense, analogy and experience. The revolution sought by the new education starts from first principles which are unfavorable to the best morals and to the soundest learning.

As a rule, the freshman, at the age of 17 or 18, has not formed his plan of life. He is too young to do so wisely. His ruling desire is to make study as light as possible and to have as good a time as possible. Now, when the new education says to such a one: "Here are two hundred groups of studies, of which you must pursue only sixteen to gain your diploma; select such as suit your preference; furthermore, follow your own option about attending recitations; you shall graduate if you mark fifty per cent. on the average," what will the average freshman do? It goes without saying, that he will choose those studies which are most to his taste, and which will cost him the least labor. You would have done it when a freshman. I should have done it when a freshman. And, again, if we had had our option about attendance, we should have gone nutting in the fall, skating in the winter and fishing in the spring, when we ought to have been in the recitation room. Out upon the notion, that the way to make a thinker of a thoughtless boy is to let him choose such studies as he pleases. Out upon the notion, that the way to make that unstable character stable is, to let the youth "cut" his recitations whenever he pleases. Some of the most valuable mental discipline in college comes from being obliged to master branches for which there is no natural liking. Some of the most valuable traits of character are the outgrowth of habits of punctuality and orderly effort formed in obedience to college requirements. What the young men of this generation need is, not encouragement to gratify their own fancy, and consult their own convenience, but to overcome the disagreeable, and to be on time when duty calls. First, make sure that these practices have become fixed principles. Then, and not until then, is it expedient to introduce electives. Let prescription govern the first half of the curriculum. Combine prescription with election during the second half, giving an ever-increasing proportion to election.

"But," replies an apostle of the new education, "the experience of Harvard overthrows these positions. The remarkable prosperity of the institution bears witness to the wisdom of the present method." That does not follow. Harvard has the prestige of two hundred and fifty years. She numbers her graduates by thousands. She feels the mighty momentum of many generations. The growth of her endowments and the multiplication of her students would have been essentially the same, under either the old system or the new.

The improvement in manliness at Harvard is sometimes urged in favor of the new education. But there is also an improvement in manliness in all the colleges of the country, no matter what the system. Within the past two or three years I have had rare opportunities to compare large bodies of students at Princeton, Amherst, Williams, Yale, and Harvard, and I have no hesitation in saying, that the manliest fellows were not Harvard men.

An enthusiastic advocate of the new system triumphantly parades the higher marking under the present method, as conclusive proof of its superiority. But what teacher does not know that marks will rise as a matter of course, wherever students are permitted to choose their own studies and instructors. There will always be a rush to the "soft" branches and to the high markers. Nothing could be more absurd than to make a grand flourish over a fact so easily explained in another way.

Once more, we are told that the average student in the upper classes at Harvard absents himself from only sixteen per cent. of his recitations. The figures are not given for the lower classes, in which the percentage of absences would be much higher. But, suppose that we should take sixteen per cent. as the average for the whole course, it would reveal to us this startling fact, that half of the students at Harvard are constantly absenting themselves from recitations one-sixth of the time. It may be fairly taken for granted that there are scores of young men in the institution who do not report for duty more than two days in three. Can you conceive of anything much worse in its influence upon scholarship and character, than the utter looseness of this optional theory and practice, during that period when mental and moral gristle is turning into bone? Now, if you will consult the better colleges, where courses are prescribed, and where attendance is required, you will find that the average of absences will be from three to six per cent., instead of sixteen per cent. or more. To which system is it safer to intrust your son at the age of seventeen or eighteen?

These figures and arguments adduced in the name of the new education are the best that she has to offer. They are taken from statistics concerning the upper classes, where we all grant that the elective and optional principles should be admitted under certain restrictions. Concerning the lower classes, about which the chief conflict rages, we are offered fancies instead of figures, and assumptions instead of arguments. The old education has abundantly proved her efficiency. She points proudly to the illustrious men whom she has trained for the service of the race, generation after generation, for centuries. There is no vocation in life which her sons have not adorned with splendid achievement. The new education has no history. She can bring forward no substantial evidence, until she can exhibit to us a race of graduates who are doing in the world grander work than that accomplished by those who have been trained in the way of the fathers. We have shown the natural tendency of her method in the case of the immature boy. We have examined what she claims as encouraging results. We have seen that all real advances are enjoyed as well under the old régime. We have shown that her own figures tell against her a damaging story in other directions.

In conclusion: If I were compelled to choose between *all* electives and *no* electives in a college course, I should say, without a moment's hesitation, *no* electives. An institution with small classes, which has sufficient funds to sustain a faculty of ten able men, and to offer three wisely selected prescribed courses, is, for legitimate *college* work, about as well off without electives as with them, even for the upper classes. Such electives are desirable, when the institution can afford them, without crippling resources needed for regular requirements, or without seriously increasing the expenses of the student.

In one way Harvard is doing great damage to strictly college education throughout the United States. She is most zealously using the vast influence which she, as the oldest and most famous seat of learning in the republic, has been acquiring for two hundred and fifty years, to make sixty millions of people believe, that any college which does not substitute optionalism for prescription is conducted on false principles, and that any college which can not furnish the most abundant electives, from matriculation to graduation, is offering a meager and comparatively worthless college education. I have no fear, however, that she will accomplish the universal revolution which she intends. The great majority of our colleges will suffer seriously for a season. They will experiment with optionals, and strain themselves to provide electives, for the sake of attracting patronage and asserting their relative importance. In so doing they will add greatly to the cost, without adding greatly to the value of the college course. But I believe that the strong common-sense of the American people will finally come to the rescue, will assert that a boy is not a man, that there is a fundamental difference between the college method and the university method, and that the college method is the method for the boy, the university method the method for the man.